To

Owolabi

There is no obstacle to great that You cant. over come. You will make it in life

19/9/10

C000127263

You Can be Richer Than Your Parents

Patricia Orlunwo Ikiriko

You can be
RICHER

than your parents

Patricia Orlunwo Ikiriko

You Can be Richer Than Your Parents

Patricia Orlunwo Ikiriko

First published in 2010 by Ecademy Press
48 St Vincent Drive, St Albans, Herts, AL1 5SJ

info@ecademy-press.com
www.ecademy-press.com

Printed and Bound by Lightning Source in the UK and USA

Set in Warnock Pro by Emma Lewis and Karen Gladwell

Cover design by Michael Inns

Printed on acid-free paper from managed forests.

This book is printed on demand, so no copies will be remaindered
or pulped.

ISBN 978-1-905823-90-1

The right of Patricia Orlunwo Ikiriko to be identified as the author
of this work has been asserted in accordance with sections 77 and
78 of the Copyright Designs and Patents Act 1988.

A CIP catalogue record for this book is available from the
British Library.

All rights reserved. No part of this work may be reproduced in
any material form (including photocopying or storing in any
medium by electronic means and whether or not transiently or
incidentally to some other use of this publication) without the
written permission of the copyright holder except in accordance
with the provisions of the Copyright, Designs and Patents Act
1988. Applications for the Copyright holder's written permission
to reproduce any part of this publication should be addressed to
the publishers.

Copyright © 2010 Patricia Orlunwo Ikiriko

Acknowledgements

This book would not have been possible without the help of my darling loving husband Hope Odhuluma Ikiriko who supported me more than words can say, Mr and Mrs Apampa who assisted me on every step in making my dream come true and Clinton Dan Jumbo my legal adviser who encouraged me every inch of the way. I am eternally grateful to my lovely children Doxa and Chanan Ikiriko for their show of understanding as I shared my attention between them and this work. In addition, I want to thank Tracey, Tricia and Grace Dixon for their moral support; my sweet mother Mrs Agnes Addey, my late dad Mark Joseph Addey and my granny Mrs Rebecca Bennet for the great seed of hard work they taught me, Rune and Blessing for editing part of the manuscript and Mindy Gibbins-Klein the Book Midwife who ensured the safe delivery of this great master piece of work. Finally, my gratitude goes to God almighty for the inspiration and knowledge he gave me to complete this humble masterpiece.

Contents

Contents

Introduction

Looking beyond your background

For every person born into our world, all possibilities exist. A life of happiness, achievement and personal fulfilment are attainable. For some, the treasures of life are stacked before them from the time they are born, for others the climb towards them will be difficult and arduous. No story illustrates this better than the one that concerns a little boy called Thomas. Tom lived with his mother and father at the foot of the Blue Ridge Mountains, Virginia, in the USA. It was a hard existence and Tom's father just scraped a living from hunting. Tom's father began to drink and one terrible night in the middle of a severe snowstorm, fought with Tom's mother, beat her and disappeared into the night, dragging her unconscious body with him, and they were never seen again.

Tom was left completely alone. His uncle lived a mile away and Tom walked barefoot through driving snow to tell him what had happened. His uncle and aunt could not take him in, having six children of their own, but agreed that he could eat his meals with them in exchange for chores around their smallholding. So each day the 10-year-old would come home from school, do chores for his uncle and then return to his cabin alone. In the morning, he would walk five miles to school when he finished working for his uncle. Tom realised early that if he was to amount to anything, his escape lay in study and he was determined that he would become someone.

His teacher was unused to any ambition from the mountain folk she taught, but recognised something in Tom, giving him catch-up sheets to make up for the schooling he missed when he was working for his uncle. As he grew, Tom was expected to shoulder more and more of the work for his uncle. In addition, he frequently slept only four hours a night, spending his time studying by candle light. Such was his determination that he used every spare moment to study. Eventually his teacher put him forward for a scholarship and he attended university to become a doctor.

Determined that his education would benefit his own people, Tom then set his sights on opening a clinic in the mountain area that he came from. He worked every spare moment to pay for his living expenses, never losing sight of his goal. Finally, he graduated with no doubt in his mind of what he wanted to do. He was determined to work with the people of his community, especially the children, trying to ensure all had the opportunities that he did not have.

Thirty years from the day that the 10-year-old Tom first found himself alone in his cabin, a hospital, nestled at the foot of the mountains, bore his name. His own children wanted for nothing, but he had not lost sight of where he came from. Every morning, before he went to work, Tom drove up into the mountains to pick up those children in the remotest places and deliver them to the school that also bears his name. His life was still one of hard work but he had achieved what he set out to achieve, and was truly fulfilled.

Tom's story shows us that a dream and a vision for our future may not be enough to deliver our goals to us— hard work and tools to help us on our way are always going to be necessary. Besides, the amazing thing is: through renewing your mind and your thought processes, you can work towards moulding yourself into the person and the place that you want to be, regardless of the circumstances you start from. By opening your mind to all possibilities and not limiting yourself by setting self-imposed barriers you can achieve what you want, and, more importantly, what you deserve. Keep your vision ahead of you at all times and in all that you do, work towards it. Set achievable targets that get you closer, systematically to where you want to be, and remain focused at all times on your ultimate objective.

Bear in mind that you did not determine where you come from and the circumstances in which you find yourself in life, and you can only determine how you end up either poor or rich. Not all fingers are equal; it is the same with your starting points, every individual starts life at different level and is good at different talents. Nevertheless, remember that your destiny is not determined by where you started, you can make every place a starting point towards a better life.

Develop a mindset of a winner and exchange what you have for what you want by making little alterations in your habits and choose to create differences, you will always attract the right opportunities you need, when you need them.

In setting a positive frame of mind, use only positive words to speak to yourself and to others. This positivity will move you forwards and upwards to the next level of your journey to success. Moreover, as you progress, more resources will become available to you. Keep in your mind, in your every waking moment, the focus of your dreams. Take as your role models those who have made it from nothing, and never let your enthusiasm grow dim. Feed it daily with hard work and study, and believe in the determination to be the best, no matter how hard the road that you have to travel. Always be flexible, do not bang your head against a brick wall, adapt, change and find ways over and around that brick wall but keep your eyes on the prize and it will be yours.

If you are a religious or spiritual person, put your faith in a higher power, give your troubles to Him and wait for your sign and direction to become clear to you. The biggest hurdle you may face is to break your way out of the little box that limits your ambition and your aims, to shake free of the little voice that tells you 'things aren't so bad, why not just settle for this?' This is a dangerous message. Your life will only be lived once; you have a duty to make a difference both to yourself and to others, and to the world you live in.

You have a debt to repay for your life and breath, and you have a responsibility to yourself to be the very best that you can be.

There is a champion inside you, which will help you to broaden your horizons, help you to shoulder your responsibilities, and, best of all, aim for what seems impossible and achieve it! In addition, your new way of thinking begins with your family, your background and your social standing. Don't be limited by any of these, rather be empowered by them to break through the invisible barriers they present to you, break free of poverty, prejudice and the limitations set by society, make the whole world your society and the world's people your family, take advice from those who speak wisely and deal fairly with everyone you meet.

Aspiration: Oprah Winfrey's Story

There is perhaps one person to whom all that we have said applies: a woman who succeeded despite, rather than because of, her background. A woman who, according to what society expects, should never have amounted to anything, and should have lived her life in a world where violence and abuse passed from generation to generation. That woman is Oprah Winfrey, the star of her own show, known worldwide, a prominent businesswoman and a philanthropist. Her experience has inspired her to give a voice to children who need protection. Yet the beginning of her life was possibly as hard as it gets.

Oprah Winfrey was born into rural poverty in the South of the United States where to be black still meant to be suppressed and even abused by a white majority where lack of opportunity and prospects were accepted as the lot of the black man and woman. Winfrey herself said, *"Nobody had any clue that my life could be anything more than a life spent working in a factory or in cotton field in Mississippi."* But the young Oprah Winfrey had other plans.

 Born in Kosciusko, Mississippi, to teenage parents, Oprah was reared by her grandmother on a farm where she set out on the course of her career by learning to read aloud and to perform recitations from the age of three. From age six to 13, Oprah lived in Milwaukee with her mother. It was not a happy time for the young Oprah, as she suffered abuse and molestation. Her mother was always working and had no time for Oprah. She did not understand this and things got worse for her as, left alone in the house, she was first raped by a cousin when she was nine years old and later molested by a male friend of her mother's and also by an uncle. Let those words sink in for a minute.

We have become used to hearing this sort of thing, almost hardened to it, maybe, but stop and think: Nine years old and raped. That is forced to lie down as a man forces his way between your legs in an act that you have no idea even exists but that you know instinctively is wrong, painful and humiliating. At nine years old? The horror and the fear must have been immense, and then the guilt that followed and the knowledge that the one person you should be able to go to, your mother, has no time for you. How does a nine-year-old come back from that? Look at your nine-year-old, cast your memory back to when you were nine years old, then try to imagine how you would be after that, when all your hopes and trust had been ground into the dirt.

Like many girls, the young Oprah never told anyone about the abuse that she was suffering. Instead, she held her anger and pain inside and she rebelled. She repeatedly ran away and got into trouble and having been sexualised at such an early age, in a pattern familiar to those dealing with children of sexual abuse, Oprah became promiscuous. Her plans for her future were unravelling, she was sliding fast down the slippery path to a wasted life and expectations for her future were bleak. Tiring of her daughter's difficult behaviour, her mother sent Oprah to be admitted to a juvenile detention home and as if this were not bad enough when she arrived Oprah was denied admission because all the beds were filled.

With no other options, she was sent to Nashville to live with her father. A strict disciplinarian, Vernon Winfrey saw to it that his daughter obeyed the curfews he set, and he also insisted that she read a book and write a book report each week. ""As strict as he was," Oprah says, "he had some concerns about me making the best of my life, and would not accept anything less than what he thought was my best." However, before she had given up her promiscuous and wild ways Oprah fell pregnant at the age of 14. We can only imagine how horrified both Oprah and her father were, but worse was to come. Oprah delivered a stillborn son, the sorrow of which still haunts her today. It was, she said, in this darkest hour that she decided that she was going to change her life, change the path of her destiny, set her mind and her heart on her goals.

Oprah Winfrey had her first break in broadcasting at age 17, when she was hired by WVOL radio in Nashville, and two years later she was taken on by WTVF-TV in Nashville as a reporter also undertaking anchor duties. She enrolled at Tennessee State University, where she majored in Speech Communications and Performing Arts.

In 1976, she moved to Baltimore to join WJZ-TV news as a co-anchor, and in 1978, Oprah first discovered her amazing talent for hosting talk shows when she became co-host of WJZ-TV's *People Are Talking.*

In January 1984, she came to Chicago to host WLS-TV's *AM Chicago*, at that time a failing local talk show. In less than 12 months, Oprah had turned AM Chicago into the hottest show in town. The format was soon given a one-hour slot and in September 1985 it was renamed *The Oprah Winfrey Show.* Seen nationally since September 8, 1986, *The Oprah Winfrey Show* became the number one talk show in national syndication in less than a year. In June 1987, in its first year of eligibility, *The Oprah Winfrey Show* received numerous awards and Oprah herself received the International Radio and Television Society's Broadcaster of the Year Award. She was the youngest person and only the fifth woman ever to receive the honour in the society's 25-year history. Anyone who, like me, had their first experience of talk shows through *The Oprah Winfrey Show* will appreciate why she became so popular so quickly.

Looking at her interacting with the people on her show, feeling their pain, sharing their triumphs, it was obvious how committed she was to understanding people, giving them a chance to be heard, giving them the encouragement and confidence that life had knocked out of them.

Moreover, she spoke for all of us when she confronted those who would abuse children, and rob others of their peace of mind and their goals. She had been there, she had been an ignored child, an abused child, a mother of a dead baby, and her empathy shone out like a beacon.

However, even before America fell in love with Oprah Winfrey and her talk show she had captured the nation's attention with her stunning portrayal of Sofia in Steven Spielberg's 1985 adaptation of *The Color Purple*, a novel by Alice Walker.

Winfrey's performance earned her nominations for an Oscar and Golden Globe Award in the category of Best Supporting Actress and her performance in *Native Son*, a movie adaptation of Richard Wright's classic 1940 novel was also hailed by critics.

In 1991, motivated in part by her own memories of childhood abuse, she started a campaign to create a national database of convicted child abusers, and testified before a U.S. Senate Judiciary Committee on behalf of a National Child Protection Act. President Clinton signed the 'Oprah Bill' into law in 1993, establishing the national database that is now available to law enforcement agencies and anyone else who is concerned, throughout the country.

She never lost sight of her dreams and despite her circumstances was determined that she would achieve the goals that she had set for herself. Winfrey had realised early that the way out of poverty was through education. Not bad for a little black girl born into poverty in the Deep South! Oprah is also an influential book critic and Academy Award-nominated actress and a magazine publisher. And from a little girl from a very unpromising start Oprah has become the richest African American of the 20th century, once even the only black billionaire! Perhaps more importantly, she has also been nominated as the most philanthropic.

As far as influence goes, Oprah has been ranked the world's most influential woman. Her struggle to succeed against the odds and her steadfast belief in herself have truly inspired millions of women and men to hold their heads up and look beyond their circumstances, to have a dream, to hold to that dream and to make their life what they want it to be. Oprah proves that the circumstances into which we are born need not define the rest of our life's expectations. All we have to do is to believe in ourselves, stay true to our dreams and work tirelessly and we too can be anything that we want to be.

All of us will face times in our lives when obstacles make our struggle more difficult and tempt us to give up the fight for what we want. It is at these times that strength and a strong mindset will pull you through and on towards your goal. You have a choice to accept or reject what challenges are before you, and determine whether to make a change.

Survival in life is like being in a flight hijacked by terrorists, where the pilots have been killed, and you are forced to take over the pilot's position to land the flight. You have to be willing to make the right decision on time if you want to survive.

In order to succeed in life you need to have dreams and aspirations, be courageous, stand for what you believe and desire to achieve, and realise that you have all it takes to step up and revolutionize your situations, and rewrite the history of your generations from poverty to SUCCESS.

Chapter One

Created to reign, succeed and excel

Decision

Decision decides your future. The decision you make today serves as the solid foundation in which your success lays. In life, you have to make decisions and commit to seeing them through. An effective way of becoming successful is making and strategizing to actualise your decision-making. Successful people develop the skill of making the best decision possible with the best information possible in the timeliest manner. They are swift to decide and quick to take responsibility for their decisions be it positive or negative. Losers put off decisions and rarely keep commitments made. However, they do not like to take a step to make decisions, hoping their life circumstances will go away on their own or they think others will take care of their future; in most cases, they blame other people for their lives.

Follow the path of successful people and learn that action is the vital key, and be conscious that procrastination kills. In the pursuit of live authenticity of consequences, know there will always be uncertainty in decisions. There is no one on earth that can see all possible ramifications; no one can predict every contingency; no one can absolutely prevent failure. Always know that failure is not final, it is a learning process and opportunity to grow and learn to know more. By taking an organized approach, you are less likely to miss important factors, and you can build on the approach to make your decisions better and better.

The genuine menace surrounding decision-making is not, 'will I make the wrong decision?' But, 'did I make the best decision possible given the facts and circumstances?' Successful people will always recover from poor decisions because they learn from their mistakes and become wiser. Nevertheless, losers will mess around and miss opportunities that are before them and mess up life opportunities and their future. In addition, once they finally make a decision, chances are their decision will have no drive, no enthusiasm and no importance to its actualisation. Learn to understand the process decisions must go through to be effective. This is the only way you can avoid the mistakes made by unsuccessful people.

To actualise your dream, learn to approach decision-making with some foundational strategies, encourage critical thinking and information-sharing skills, understand the rationale for the decision, dig deeper, and look at the problem from different angles. If you use the mindset that there must be other solutions out there, you are more likely to make the best decision possible if the decision is likely to work in the long term.

What makes a man great is within him, keep in mind that greatness is not determined by age, size, background, height or resources available to him, but founded on the decision he is able to make to pursue his dreams and aspirations in life. Some take the vital step from an early age.

Some great men are born, some acquire greatness, and some have greatness entrusted on them, but their decision to take responsibility helps them to blossom and remain great. Great men in our generation like a man well-known today in the world of soccer —Cristiano Ronaldo could be used to illustrate the bold step of decision-making from an early age.

Cristiano Ronaldo's Story

Ronaldo, from a very tender age, made the decision of what he wanted in life. His passion and drive are his goal-scoring which made him stand out, football fans love this and look out for who will use them in that moment of joy and excitement. He passionately devotes his time and training to enhance his goal-scoring ability. He quoted in his own words; *"goal scoring is everything to me"*, and this involves a lot of skill, he is determined to put in his best at achieving his desire. Decision-making is one of the master keys that ushered him into the hall of fame, and gained him favour before men.

Cristiano Ronaldo was born in Funchal, Madeira on 5 February 1985. He is the last son of Jose Diniz Aveiro and the kit man for a soccer team called Andorinha, and he has two sisters and one brother. He grew up in a small house in the city of Funchal and began playing soccer for a youth team in Madeira, where his dad was the team's equipment manager.

The young kid from Madeira was never interested in studies in his childhood. In school, Ronaldo (he received this name as a tribute to former US president Ronald Reagan) did not like to study and the only time he really worked hard was at mealtimes when he and his pals used to play football all the time. Ronaldo in his early days was rejected by a team called The Flamengo in his home town in Brazil. He was rejected not because he could not play, but because he did not have enough money to pay his bus fare for training. His father, an alcoholic, had lost his job and did not have any money to support his fare. His mother Sonia, who was a waitress in a pizza restaurant at that time, didn't want to finance her son to play soccer; her desire for him was to be better-educated as is every good mum's dream for their children.

Nevertheless, Cristiano Ronaldo refused to succumb to this pressure to give up his dreams and aspirations; rather, he made a decision to follow his heart to do only what he knew he could do best to realise his God-given purpose on earth. He had a great desire, determination, drive and confidence. At an early age, he was quoted to have boldly declared, *"I will become the best footballer in the world. I will be rich and help my family."* He had such passion for the ball that it led him to Clube Futebol Andorinha de Santo Antonio — where his father used to work. Later, he went to the amateur league of Nacional da Ilha da Madeira, in 1995. In his first year at Nacional, Ronaldo won the kids' championship, going to Lisbon at only 11 years old.

Ronaldo has gone from a small island in the middle of the ocean to the top of the soccer world. In Lisbon, he played for Sporting Lisbon as a youth. In September of 2002, the kid from Madeira Island started his professional career for the Sporting Lisbon pro club team, when he was only 17 years old.

In the 2002/2003 season, Ronaldo played 25 games for the club, scoring three goals. In the inaugural match of the new José Alvalade stadium (Sporting's stadium that was renovated for Euro 2004), Ronaldo played a terrific match against Manchester United. With this great performance, United's players asked Sir Alex Ferguson to sign the Portuguese guy as substitute for the superstar David Beckham.

In 2003, Ronaldo signed a contract with Manchester United, where he made United's fans quickly forget David Beckham. With a great squad, Chelsea started its dynasty in England, winning the Premier League in that year. But Ronaldo was known as a great revelation with the number 7 jersey. This number is magical for the Manchester side — three of the main legends in the history of the club had the number 7 on the back (George Best, Eric Cantona and David Beckham).

After a not-so-brilliant start, Ronaldo started little by little to honour the number 7. He scored goal number 1000 in the Premiership for Manchester United in 2005. In 2006, he scored in the Carling Cup Final and helped to win the trophy. But at last the world could see what this Portuguese boy could do. Cristiano Ronaldo finally won a Premiership title with the Red Devils. Elected the best player in England for the 2006/2007 season, Cristiano Ronaldo was the 'key' for Manchester United's Championship after four years and finishing Chelsea's dynasty. Besides, he took United to the semis of the UEFA Champions League, when a painful loss to Milan ended the dream of the third trophy.

In 2008, Ronaldo won his first UEFA Champions League title, and was named player of the tournament. He was named the FIFPro World Player of the Year and the FIFA World Player of the Year, in addition to becoming Manchester United's first Ballon d'Or winner in 40 years. Three-time Ballon d'Or winner Johan Cruyff said in an interview on 2 April 2008, *"Ronaldo is better than George Best and Denis Law,"* who were two brilliant and great players in the history of United.

In 2009, he broke a Madrid club record when he scored in a league match against Villareal and thus became the first ever player to score in his first four La Liga appearances. He made the best decision and won his price to the limelight.

Find your passion in life and face it, never run away, decide and go through the desert. Do not be afraid to make critical decisions to succeed, focus and face your delicate situation, appraise it and do not discount it. Always calculate what it will cost you and bear in mind the end should be your main goal. Make up your mind and put in your best ability as Ronaldo did to bring your change forever. Define and decide what you want to achieve, for determining the most appropriate way of making the decision will help you address the critical elements that result in a good decision.

Remember, your decision determines your altitude in life.

Determination

One of the master keys you need that can help you take the bold step that will change your life forever is determination.

Determination is an interesting word, a word that makes us think of someone hard-headed, even forceful, someone who has his sights on what he wants and is going for it, no matter what. We can see it in the baby's determination to take his first step, as the child determined to do well in his sport, to score that goal, and as the adult determined to make a better life for himself and his family.

For someone from a poorer background, where everything seems to be stacked against their ever having the chance to succeed, determination is going to be the tool they use to slowly but surely ease their way out of their situation. Determination is going to be the strength that you find to go on when everything around you makes it easier to give up, determination is going to be what eventually gets you to where you deserve to be. You have to be determined to succeed, and you have to know what that word represents; sacrifice, not giving in to weakness, being set on your path and not being swayed from your goals. It is a mindset that, if followed every hour of every day, will deliver to you your hard-won prize, whatever that may be.

So what if your background is ok, you have no particular burdens to shake off, or obstacles to overcome? Does that make you soft and take away the urgency, the desire, the determination to do better? If you are already comfortable can you become complacent? Of course you can! Is it possible that every now and then an individual is touched by some greater force and seems to be created to succeed, to lead or to excel? Does that person then not have to work? Will everything just fall in their lap? Do they need determination and vision as well? Do you?

Donald John Trump's Story

Donald John Trump is a name familiar to most people in the world. He is known as a man of immense wealth who seems to go from strength to strength. So it looks like it has all been plain sailing for Donald John Trump then, born into a well-to-do family? Well, no. In fact, there is no argument that Trump's businesses have been in and out of bankruptcy proceedings since the early 1990s. One example, The Taj Mahal Casino, which Trump financed largely with high-interest junk bonds, was forced into bankruptcy and, in 1992, the Trump Plaza Hotel was forced to reorganise under a Chapter 11 bankruptcy plan after being unable to meet its debt payments. And once again in 2004, Trump Hotels was forced to file for Chapter 11 bankruptcy. This would be enough to finish most men, but what did Donald John Trump have to say about his bankruptcies? Well, he said; *"I don't think it's a failure, it's a success."* This is an important point for us all to take on board. Failure is a state of mind. Obviously not a state of mind that Donald John Trump has much trouble in converting to positivism! Trump was determined not to let setbacks sway him from his success, and they never have. Every time he has been knocked down he has got up again, twice as strong and more determined than ever!

It is obvious that someone in Oprah Winfrey's position has nothing to lose and everything to gain by fighting for their dreams and aspirations, but what about someone like Donald John Trump? Donald John Trump's father was a successful real estate business owner and Trump's upbringing was comfortable, even privileged. He started his career in an office he shared with his father, Fred, in Sheepshead Bay, Brooklyn, New York. Trump and his father worked together for five years, when they collaborated on doing deals on numerous projects. Donald John Trump has always given his father credit for being his mentor from whom he learned a tremendous amount about every aspect of the real estate and construction industry. Fred C. Trump, Donald's father, in turn gives his son credit for doing some of the best deals, likening him to Midas, the Greek king where everything he touched seemed to turn to gold. So it was from these promising beginnings Trump turned his attention to the very much higher stakes of Manhattan real estate.

Today, in New York City, the Trump signature is associated with the most prestigious of addresses. Among them is the world-recognised Fifth Avenue skyscraper, Trump Tower. Some of the other luxurious residential buildings that Donald John Trump has been responsible for include the Trump World Tower at the United Nations Plaza, Trump Park Avenue at 59th Street and Park Avenue, Trump Place on the Hudson River and Trump Palace. In 1997, Trump International Hotel & Tower opened its doors to the world, a 52-storey super luxury hotel and residential building designed by the famed architect Philip Johnson.

Donald John Trump is also well known in the golfing world as a first class course developer, with award-winning courses in New York, New Jersey, Los Angeles, Palm Beach, Canouan Island in the Grenadines and one that has just opened in Aberdeen, Scotland as well as Puerto Rico and the Dominican Republic. Donald John Trump is himself an avid golfer and his passion is obvious in the spectacular courses he has developed and continues to develop worldwide.

As an accomplished and best-selling author, Donald John Trump has drawn on his own experience and philosophy for life and has had numerous best sellers including *The Art of the Deal*, that is considered a business classic, a work that has inspired so many, and *The Art of the Comeback*, *The America We Deserve*, *How To Get Rich*, *Think Like a Billionaire*, *Trump 101*, *Why We Want You To Be Rich*, *Think Big*, *Never Give Up*, and *Think Like a Champion*. All excellent messages for all of us!

True to the old saying that 'success breeds success' and in a departure from his real estate triumphs, Trump and the NBC Television Network have become partners in the ownership and the broadcasting rights for the Miss Teen USA, Miss USA and Miss Universe Pageants. In January of 2004, Trump joined forces with Mark Burnett Productions and NBC to produce and star in the television reality show, *The Apprentice*. We have to ask ourselves, who else would they choose? The show that has had success worldwide stormed to number one in the ratings and is now enjoying its eighth season. Donald John Trump's production company, Trump Productions, is based in Los Angeles. And as if this TV success was not enough, Donald John Trump also has a successful radio program on Clear Channel, which he has had for several years.

Donald J. Trump is the very epitome of the American success story. He has, time after time, set new standards of excellence and has succeeded in expanding his interests nationally and internationally and over many diverse areas. His success has come in many different fields of endeavour and the only common denominator in all of it is the man himself. This proves what we can do if we set our minds to it, if we believe in ourselves, refuse to take no for an answer and accept no imposed limits to our success.

What is more, Donald John Trump is personally involved in everything that bears his name. This is the kind of commitment that has made him the pre-eminent developer of the most desired real estate, known all around the world, and in everything that he undertakes that famous Trump gold standard is very much in evidence. He is the archetypal businessman — a deal maker without equal and additionally is an ardent philanthropist. However, this kind of commitment and attention to detail is what will make you succeed. Even when you think things are fine, when you think that you have made it, do not take your eye off the ball, because if you do you risk losing touch with the mindset and the determined attitude that you have so carefully nurtured and utilised for your success.

Donald John Trump can teach you a lot about fulfilling your potential and your dreams. I believe that some of his sayings are worth learning by heart and keeping as a mantra to help you through the times when your resolve falters and you lose sight of your goals, sayings like:

- *Anyone who thinks my story is anywhere near over is sadly mistaken.*

- *As long as you're going to be thinking anyway, think big.*

- *Experience taught me a few things. One is to listen to your gut, no matter how good something sounds on paper. The second is that you're generally better off sticking with what you know. And the third is that sometimes your best investments are the ones you don't make.*

- *I don't make deals for the money. I've got enough, much more than I'll ever need. I do it to do it.*

- *I try to learn from the past, but I plan for the future by focusing exclusively on the present. That's where the fun is.*

- *I wasn't satisfied just to earn a good living. I was looking to make a statement.*

- *If you're interested in 'balancing' work and pleasure, stop trying to balance them. Instead make your work more pleasurable.*

Donald John Trump

Moreover, this is the secret. Do not allow failure or set back to cloud your vision; do not give in to dejection and hopelessness. Pick yourself up and dust yourself off and have another go. If you truly can alter your mindset to see failure as success, or at least a platform from which to build future success you can learn from it and make your way forward, you will succeed, you can't fail! You could be someone 'created to reign', to excel and succeed against all the odds. All you need is faith in yourself and belief that you are that person. The only limitations to your success are the ones that you impose.

Be possibility-minded, do not limit your aspirations or put a ceiling on what is possible. Everything is possible if you believe it is. Whether you started out in life with an advantage, or not, your mindset and your spirit are yours forever, no one can take that from you and you can use them how you like. You can use them to make excuses for yourself, as to why a goal is unattainable, why you will never be as rich as he will, as fulfilled as her, or you can use them to open all the possibility in the world to yourself. Deny yourself no opportunity, never be afraid to look behind any closed door, believe in your destiny to be excellent, successful and a leader of men, and you will be. Develop the mind of strong warriors who never give up until they win. Be strong and courageous and you will surely get there.

Usain Bolt's Story

What must it be like to be the fastest man on the planet, and how much determination do you need to win that title? Well Usain Bolt knows, endowed as he is with that incredible title and the determination it took to get it.

Usain St. Leo Bolt was born on 21 August 1986 and grew up in Trelawny, Jamaica, with his parents, Jennifer and Wellesley Bolt, and his sister Sherine. Usain expressed a love for dancing as a young boy, which fits with the most frequent description of his character as relaxed, laid back, a truly chilled individual! In fact the first sport that Usain became involved in was cricket and he said if he wasn't a sprinter he would be a fast bowler instead. But when he first attended

William Knibb Memorial High School, his cricket coach noticed Bolt's speed on the pitch and directed him to try track and field events.

Pablo McNeil and Dwayne Barrett coached Bolt, encouraging him to focus his energy on improving his athletic abilities. William Knibb Memorial High School had an impressive history of athletic success with past students including Michael Green. Usain went on to win his first annual high school championships medal, and young Usain grew to be 6'5, much taller than anyone who had ever been successful in sprinting. It was thought that he was too tall and too bulky ever to succeed in his chosen discipline. Now you would imagine that in a sport where 100ths of a second count and physical attributes and prowess are very rigidly prescribed, that that would be the end of that.

However, it seems that the laid-back boy from Jamaica who liked to dance had other ideas, and this really took determination. After being told that he could not possibly hope to succeed by the brightest and the best in that sport, he went ahead anyway. It is hard to imagine the young Bolt taking on the combined opinion of his elders and leaders but he was determined to prove them wrong. Nevertheless, prove them wrong he did! Usain Bolt's achievements make impressive and awe-inspiring reading. He did not earn the nickname Lightning Bolt for nothing; I am not going to document the long and illustrious list of titles and world records he has smashed.

I am more interested in what drives the man, or any man to be a success. Was Usain simply born to succeed? Could nothing have stopped him from getting to where he is today? Was his fate sealed the day he was born? Well maybe, and the physical abilities he went on to demonstrate certainly had an organic beginning. Moreover, if Usain had continued with cricket at school, no doubt he would have been just as much a sensation as he has proved to be in athletics.

If ever there was an example of a boy born to succeed in his field, Usain is it! In addition, that laid-back persona, do not let it fool you, no one gets to the level that Usain has without hours and days and years of preparation, hard work, effort and determination. This is an excellent example of how starting with a talent or being born to succeed can lead you to be the best. Being quick to realise your talent, working hard to perfect it and being willing to take advice is also important. If Usain had not taken the advice of his cricket coach, he may have been a great cricketer but missed being an even greater runner. On the other hand if he had taken the advice of those who told him that he was too tall, or too big to succeed as a sprinter, we would never has seen his breathtaking performance on the track. Be flexible while you keep your eyes on your goal.

In life, do not dismiss any opportunity that comes along; learn to capitalise on those opportunities and to assess possibilities. Develop strong instincts for which way is best to go, which path is the one for you. Usain did this, he was determined, whatever anyone said, to be the best, and he achieved what he set out to do. While you should always listen to those who have trod the same path before you, do not let them influence you unduly. However, even if they might not have made it to where you ultimately want to be, their insight and their experience is something to be built upon. Above all, you have to believe in yourself, keep the determined attitude that started you off on your path in your sights and never waiver from it. Success is the harvest of determination, and is yours for the taking.

Chapter One

Chibuike Rotimi Amaechi's Story

How fulfilled can a man be when he achieves a breakthrough for himself, his family, his state and nation at large? Including all those who believe in his leadership and vision, after that vision suffered several threats of abortion and destruction from the hands of mortals, who plunge themselves into a ditch of multiple conspiracy in an attempt to frustrate the vision.

This was the case of the oil-rich Rivers State in the Niger Delta part of Nigeria in 2007 during the general election that brought in Rt. Hon. Rotimi C Amaechi as governor of the state. In the midst of that seeming catastrophe, the only thing that sustained the dream and vision was the determination of Rotimi Amaechi who was then the speaker of the state Assembly (Legislative House) and the legitimate candidate for the People's Democratic Party.

Self-determination is the free choice of one's own act without external compulsion. In addition, in politics, it is the liberty of the people of a particular area to determine their political status and governance without undue influence from any other person or group of persons.

The instrument he employed to actualize this apparition was just determination with a strong confidence in the rule of law. Amaechi (popularly known) was born on 27 May, 1965 to the family of late Elder and Mrs Fidelis Nsirimovu Amaechi of Mgbuelus village in Ubima Community, in Ikwerre Local Government Area of Rivers State.

A great man who has a very humble background but does not allow this to deter him from achieving any of his set goals in life as he pursues life with so much passion and diligence. Even while serving his mentor, Dr Peter Odili, as he grew through the ladder, he is one man that is known for doggedness in the protection of his mentor. This is an attitude that brought him so much hatred amongst his relatives for some saw him as a 'sell out'. His style of fellowship that is uncommon is characterized by honesty, diligence and reliability.

Amaechi as a child attended St. Teresa's Primary School, Ubima from 1970 – 1976, and then attended the Government Secondary School, Okolobiri from 1977 – 1982. Rotimi Amaechi also attended the university of Port-Harcourt, Chobe in 1983 and graduated from the department of English in 1987. He also has a master's degree in English language and linguistics from the same university.

Amaechi, who may not have attended the best schools in the world, is one personality that has so developed himself through determination and one who can proudly exhibit leadership attributes that can be compared to some world class leaders that are Harvard trained. His thinking, his I.Q, his approach to problems, his posture and his mentality for development, which has turned Rivers State overnight and put it on the path of progression is something we cannot take away from him.

Amaechi's early acquaintance and discipleship under the then governor of Rivers State Dr Peter Odili, as far back as 1988 when he served as the public relations officer of PAMO clinics (where Dr Peter Odili, his predecessor, was the medical director), offered him the required opportunity for a good foundation for his early life. A few years later, he was appointed the secretary of the now-defunct National Republican Convention (NRC) in the Ikwerre Local Government Area, which was his own local government. After the success of the general election of 1992, he was appointed the special assistant to the governor Chief Rufus Ada-George on youth affairs while also serving as personal assistant to the Deputy Governor Dr Peter Odili.

This is an uncommon achievement but for his consistent discipleship of his mentor Dr Peter Odili. He was not too ambitious but was very passionate about his job at any point in time. He could hardly say no to any assignment given to him by his superiors. He grew to become the state secretary of the now-defunct Democratic Party of Nigeria (DPD), under the tutelage of the governor Dr Peter Odili who was the then national secretary of the party.

This diligence of Rotimi Amaechi metamorphosed into his election into the Rivers State house of assembly in 1999 to represent his people of Ikwerre state constituency, an election that originally declared his opponent as the winner. Being a man full of courage and determination and who believed that the result was an aberration, he challenged this result in court and got judgement in his favour at the appeal court which brought him in as the elected member of the house assembly representing this constituency.

Amaechi, unlike many who live in Nigeria who have lost hope in the judicial system of the country, is driven by a major force called 'determination' not to allow his dream to be killed or aborted prematurely by any unholy system that could be man-made. Against all hope he believed in hope and was fully persuaded that his confidence in the rule of law will give him justice in a society that may be seen as morally bankrupt by many who have lost hope in themselves but struggle to put the blame on others or the system which they have also contributed to destroy.

After being sworn into office at the legislative Assembly, Rotimi Amaechi found favour in the sight of all his colleagues who elected him anonymously as the speaker of the Rivers State house of assembly. His poise and courage as speaker endeared him to the hearts of his colleagues who willingly became so loyal to his leadership that it earned him several awards and accolades as the best speaker in the country, a development that earned it the prestigious award as the most peaceful and coordinated house of assembly. His commitment to his work and determination to succeed showcased this to his counterparts in other states who found him fit to serve as the chairman of the conference of speakers in the county, a position he held for two terms in office even as he served as speaker for two terms also.

Throughout the period of his stay as speaker for two terms, the house did not witness any major crisis or impeachment because of his vibrant and dynamic style of leadership. His courage and determination to succeed made him to be the people's leader.

As every mortal leader, Amaechi may have his weaknesses but the force of determination inherent in him does not allow these weaknesses to overwhelm his vision and poise to enforce change around his environment. The few challenges that faced the house were confronted simultaneously by him with his usual determination to succeed. His greatest challenges were experienced towards the end of his second term in office, a period that was characterised with so much antics, manoeuvring, outwitting and power play as result of the transition that unshelled him in as the governor of the state. This again could not deter him from the show of determination, an outstanding manifestation that changed the course of the justice system of the entire nation.

However, the landmark ruling of the supreme court of the federal republic of Nigeria, a judgement that enthroned him as governor of 'new' Rivers State is the first of its kind in the history of the country that a governor is declaimed by the Supreme Court, the highest court in the land.

He faced a battle which put his spirit of determination to the test as he witnessed betrayals, abandonment, conspiracy and witchcraft of the highest order, by both friends, relatives, political associates and 'Godfathers' including his mentors. However, his determination to face the battle gave him victory in the end.

Mindset

So what is a positive mindset? How do you achieve it,
make it work for you, deliver the outcomes you want? Well
first, you de-clutter! Train yourselves to have uncluttered
thinking, and not to dwell on inconsequential things.
You focus your energy and your abilities into reinforcing
your mindset and building up the image of the way you
need to go and the tasks you need to undertake to reach
your goals. You do not limit your possibilities by limiting
your capabilities, to the man with the successful mindset,
everything is possible, and with every obstacle that he
comes to, he finds a way around it or over it. His mindset is
his compass and it is set for SUCCESS!

There can be few men who demonstrate this as well, or who
deserves our respect more than Barack Hussein Obama II
does. Here is an example of a man who set his mind on the
prize and never wavered from his course. At the time that
he was born, in 1961, the prospect of a black president of
the United States was a pretty far-fetched notion.

Barack Hussein Obama II's Story

Barack Hussein Obama II was born to a white American mother and a black Kenyan student father. His mother and her parents brought up the young Barack Hussein Obama II in Hawaii. Barack Hussein Obama II's father had left them to pursue further study and then eventually he returned to Kenya. Barack Hussein Obama II's early years were far from unhappy, but did, nevertheless, leave the boy to undertake a solitary voyage to discover his racial identity. School was a tense time for the young Barack Hussein Obama II, possibly because he was struggling with black literature.

Barack Hussein Obama II saw little of his father, apart from a month-long visit when he was 10 when he remembers his father as a commanding presence. This was a boy who had much to overcome, including, what many of us take for granted, his uncertainty about his heritage, and the inevitable questions that must have plagued him about why his father had not been more of a presence in his life. We hear a lot about children like this, the fact that they are from broken homes being blamed for any trouble they get into. But here was a boy who, from very early in his life, developed a mindset, that, while it accommodated the questions and uncertainties he had about where he came from and who he was, was able to offer the young Barack Hussein Obama II the steadfastness of purpose that he needed to succeed.

Thinking about his early childhood, Barack Hussein Obama II remembers that his father looked nothing like the people around him in that his skin was 'black as pitch' while his mother was white as milk, but this barely registered with the young boy.

Years later when Barack Hussein Obama II reflected on his formative years in Honolulu, he wrote:

Chapter One

"The opportunity that Hawaii offered to experience a variety of cultures in a climate of mutual respect, became an integral part of my world view, and a basis for the values that I hold most dear." The stumbling block and downfall of many youngsters, Barack Hussein Obama II has also written and talked about using alcohol, cannabis and even cocaine during his teenage years to push the unanswered questions about who he was out of his mind.

Years later at the Civil Forum on the Presidency held in 2008, Barack Hussein Obama II identified his high-school drug use as his "greatest moral failure." However, this shows us what a successful mindset can do. How many promising students and young people have fallen into the use of drugs or alcohol and never been able to pull themselves out, never been able to resume their chosen path, and ultimately wasted the promise that life held for them? That Barack Hussein Obama II managed to pull free and to come to terms with the issues he had, take hold of his dreams again and utilise the strength of his mind and his determination, shows us clearly what is possible.

Barack Hussein Obama II became a student of law at Harvard University and went on to become the first black president of the Harvard Law Review. After college as a civil rights lawyer, Barack Hussein Obama II became a community organizer in Chicago. He slowly found his place and a sense of purpose among people he could identify with racially despite having very different backgrounds, winning enough small victories to commit himself to the work.

Barack Hussein Obama II's father had died during this time and he decided to visit Kenya in the quest to fully understand his identity. *"Will the truth set you free?"* Barack Hussein Obama II wrote *"Or will it disappoint?"* The answer, it seems, is a bit of both. His search for himself as a black American was documented in his book *Dreams from My Father: A Story of Race and Inheritance* is a work that is rooted in the particulars of his daily life. The book also provides a wry commentary on us all. Barack Hussein Obama II has no time for labels that some would have him adopt such as a "tragic mulatto" and to illustrate his point of view, shows how much we are all subject to the messy contradictions and disparate communities around us.

Barack Hussein Obama II's trip to Kenya, the land of his father, revealed the fact that Kenya has 400 different tribes, each of them with firmly established stereotypes of the others. Barack Hussein Obama II has always been forthright in talking about the racism, poverty and corruption he found both in Chicago and in Kenya.

Barack Hussein Obama II was a man who overcame an uncertain beginning as regards his identity. Although his childhood was mostly a happy one he never stopped wanting to complete the picture, to know who his father was, what mixture of cultures made him who he was. Nonetheless, this did not become the focus of his life; instead, it enhanced him, rather than drawing his attention away from his goals. I am sure you do not need me to tell you the rest of the story of this remarkable man. He has shown that he has very human failings like all of us, and has had the strength of mind to overcome difficult issues and beat addictions to triumph and reach his goal. This was not an easy prize to win, nothing that is worth having ever comes easily, but with the right mindset, everything and anything is possible.

By the time he famously called himself 'a skinny kid with a funny name' at the 2004 Democratic National Convention, his star was already in the ascendancy and by the time he triumphed in the 2004 Illinois Senate race, he was the golden child of a Democratic party, at that time, in desperate need of a charismatic leader. In November of 2008, as the world held its breath, as he was declared the first African-American to be elected President of the United States.

This is a man who history will never let us forget, the first black American president, who has managed to bring together the different races and creeds of the United States. He is an intelligent man, a high achiever, but then many men and women are. What has made Barack Hussein Obama II succeed where others have not? Mindset and focus are words that can offer you the same unlimited success enjoyed by Barack Hussein Obama II. Very early in life Barack Hussein Obama II knew what interested him, where his passion lay and what his goal would be. He had his sights set on the big prize, the office of President of the United States; some would say the most powerful leader in the world. Not bad for a young boy of mixed parentage, who, at the time and in the place he was born, might have been expected to do something locally, but never would have been expected to achieve the highest office in the land.

The mindset of a man destined for this kind of greatness is unwavering, his determination and commitment to his goal focused and established. Nevertheless, he is not a super human, far from it; he is an ordinary boy who grew up with many of the worries and concerns that any of us have. The difference between your success and your failure, I will say it again, mindset. This is the secret. Your mind has to be made up, the contract with yourself non-negotiable, your eyes on the prize and your heart committed to your goal. If you can achieve a positive and focused mindset there is nothing you cannot achieve.

You are only limited by the limitations that you place on yourself. Open your mind to all that is necessary for you to reach your goal and keep your mind open and set and you can and will achieve all that you are capable of. Too many of us limit ourselves by what is expected of us, what is 'normal' for our social, educational or racial background. Where would Barack Hussein Obama II be if he had limited himself to enjoying the laid-back life of Hawaii, if he had not seen the bigger picture, known that he could make a difference, and contribute to his country? I can tell you, he would not be the first black President of the United States of America. So whatever your goal, understand how this mixed-race boy and his mindset delivered as his prize the highest office in the world. Whatever your aspirations, wherever you want to go and whatever you want to be, all is possible if you fix your goal before you, set your mind to embrace the hard work and endeavour that will be necessary to reach your prize and believe in YOURSELF.

Divine Grace and Steadfastness

There is a time perhaps in all lives when a man has a vision or message for his future, a visitation of divine grace, and a message that gives him a meaning for life. Many people will ignore that message and will decide instead to carry on their own way without any influence of divine grace. In everything you do, you must be sure of your message and your direction and you must hold fast to that. Steadfast belief in yourself and what you are trying to achieve is something that none of you will succeed without.

The path that you have to follow may be rocky and may look impossible but if you hold on steadfastly to your dream and allow divine grace to guide you, you will make it to your goal. Open your heart and your mind to all the possibilities that life is offering you to make the most of your life and your work and remain steadfast for a long slog. However, persistently and surely holding onto your dream will bring you to your reward. Listen for the message, the sign of what divinity and life have planned for you. Do not ignore it; it will be the single most important message of your life. One man who could not ignore the message and who, through his steadfastness, courage, diligence, wisdom and determination has made a difference to thousands of people's lives all over the world is David Olaniyi Oyedepo.

David Olaniyi Oyedepo's Story

On September 27 1954, David Olaniyi Oyedepo was born in Omu Aran, Kwara State, Nigeria, into a religiously mixed family. His father Ibrahim was a Muslim healer and his mother Dorcas was a member of the Eternal Order of the Cherubim and Seraphim Movement (C&S), a branch of the Aladura movement in Nigeria. Like many great men before him, David knew that education would be the foundation for everything he would achieve and gained a PhD in Human Development from the University of Honolulu in Hawaii.

David's life changed in May 1981 when, in an 18-hour-long vision, he had a direct message from God to 'liberate the world from all oppression of the devil through the preaching of the word of faith'. Having received his calling, David founded the Liberation Faith Hour Ministries in 1981. The divine grace that was leading him helped him to remain steadfast, and two years later David and his wife Florence were ordained as pastors and they commissioned the new church of Oyedepo. David threw himself into his work, ministering to his congregation and five years later was ordained as Bishop. His fledgling ministry went on to become the headquarters of David's church 'The Winners Chapel' and such was its popularity that people regularly spilled out onto the streets when they could not get a seat inside. Divine grace again guided David Olaniyi Oyedepo as he realized that he would have to give his congregation a bigger place to meet and worship and the now famous Faith Tabernacle was born. The auditorium of the Faith Tabernacle was reported to be the largest in the world with a 50,000 seating capacity. For such an enormous building, the speed of construction was breathtaking. Almost a mini village in its own right, the Caananland campus has businesses and banks, housing, restaurants and even a petrol station.

David has had a lifelong steadfast commitment to education, realizing that it can offer a way out of poverty and be the gateway to a successful and productive life. Steadfastly he set about building a network of nursery and primary schools, holding as his inspiration the commitment to help every child discover his or her purpose and potential, and give the best chance of becoming productive fulfilled citizens in whatever field they pursue.

Guided by divine grace in 2002, Covenant University (CU) was established. What makes this university different to others is the fact that all members, both academic and non-academic staff, are made up of Christian intellectuals and professors. In 2005, Covenant University was judged to be the best private university in Nigeria.

According to the vision of David Olaniyi Oyedepo, the campus of Covenant University displays excellence in an amazing number of architectural masterpieces, perhaps the greatest of which is the building that houses the Learning Resources (university library). If any building could epitomize the vision and the dedication of David Olaniyi Oyedepo this building in its majesty and the promise that it holds for a bright future, for all who study in it, is a shining beacon of achievement and dedication to the future of Nigeria's young people. It is hard to imagine that one man could, through steadfast effort and commitment, self-sacrifice and vision achieve all that David Olaniyi Oyedepo has achieved but Covenant University is perhaps the pinnacle of his achievements, offering as it does excellence in education as well as an assured future for the students who are lucky enough to attend there. To offer someone a future, you need to offer him or her an education. David Olaniyi Oyedepo is a man who, knowing this, has embraced this concept both for himself and for his fellow man. He truly gives a priceless gift in all his educational endeavours.

David Olaniyi Oyedepo is known by the affectionate nickname of Papa by those who follow and admire him. This is a man who has made it his life's mission to help others; and through focus on his goal and on the good, what he could do for his fellow human beings has made a real difference to the lives of countless men women and children. Such a life is one of sacrifice and of putting ones personal desires behind that of the greater good. Men prepared to do this are rare. David Olaniyi Oyedepo is one of those rare human beings who has a message, and a focus for their lives, and who have been steadfast in their commitment to their fellow man. He has been courageous, firm, faithful, focused and steadfast in all his commission. Guided by divine grace and wisdom that comes from learning and understanding, you too could achieve your life's ambitions, whatever they might be. Keep your mind and heart open to receive your message and be true in your commitment and you too can achieve a great triumph.

Chapter 2

Master Keys To Great Achievement

Goal setting

Goal setting is an essential ingredient of your success. Just like the footballer who does a triumphant run after he has scored a goal, you too need to set goals for yourself that you can feel elated about attaining. Goal setting is the signpost to your success, according to Brian Tracy, *"a wise man once told me success is goal; all else is commentary."* Conversely, to achieve great success you need clear-cut goals, and schedules to get from wherever you are today to wherever you wish to be in the near future. The feeling of achievement as your carefully executed plans and exceptional effort reward you with reaching that goal.

Success is like a journey. No one embarks on a journey to a strange land without a map or directions on how to get there. The set map gives you a clearer picture of how to prepare and a guide on necessary things needed for the trip. The set goals are a signpost that will direct you to your desired destinations.

Life is like a dream; no one can make your dream come true but you, others can only contribute to what you have made for yourself. In the book of Chronicles, Solomon, the richest man who ever lived, became successful before men brought gifts to him.

Ikiriko's Goal-setting Schedule/Tips

Goals that can make visible changes in your life need immediate short-term and long-term plans.

Tips to remember:

- D - Decide what you want
- W - Write down things you need
- S - Set a time limit
- M - Make a to-do list
- F - Follow sequential order = step by step = bricks and mortar method
- M - Make a plan
- T - Take action
- E - Evaluate and do something on your goals daily

Advancement steps could be taking daily, weekly, monthly and yearly action and effectively evaluate the goal-setting progress.

Daily, write a list of everything you want to do for the day, this will save you a lot of time and help you remain focused. Whatever you do in a day, remember to incorporate your goals at least an hour into your daily living.

Today I will:

1.

2.

3.

4.

5.

This week, I will:

   1.

   2.

   3.

   4.

   5.

Weekly, always evaluate to see that your goal plans are systematically carried out; and slot in time to work on a specific task. In addition, make sure other things are also done in your life too.

This month I will:

   1.

   2.

   3.

   4.

   5.

Monthly, assess the level of work done on your list to see the achievement you have made so far. Assess your weakness, and see where you need improvement, but never be too hard on yourself. See weaknesses as a stepping-stone in achieving your desired goals. Get more information on what you are doing, to enhance your knowledge and the process.

This year, I will:

1.

2.

3.

4.

5.

Yearly, measure the overall performance of your goals attained so far, make adjustments where possible, applaud yourself and work harder.

However, beware, set realistic goals. Nothing ensures failure more than the misery that comes from being unable to reach a goal that was unattainable. Rather, set a series of goals for you to aim for, with one leading on naturally to the next. Without setting and striving for goals, you will never reach the potential that you are capable of. The goals you set for yourself are a measure of your progress of how you are doing, of how far you have come and how far you have to go. Use short-term goals as your stepping stones to your ultimate goal, ticking each one off as you go and feeling your confidence grow with each goal you reach. Goals can be your friend, your barometer of how you are doing, the measure of your success and your way to where you want to be.

Brian Tracy's Story

Brian Tracy was not born with a silver spoon in his mouth. He grew up in a poor family and was forced to wear charity store clothes as he grew up. Perhaps predictably, as Tracy narrated in his teleconference, he dropped out of school, worked for some time in various jobs as a labourer, and unable to afford a home of his own had to live in boarding houses.

When he was 21, Tracy found work on a Norwegian freighter ship, which gave him the experience of travelling all around the world. His wanderlust satisfied, he returned eventually to the more mundane life of labouring. However, at this time he had his first taste of selling, doing a small amount of selling on commission.

Although Brian Tracy did not at first show any signs of success, in the back of his mind he had always been fascinated by the question 'What makes some people successful and others not?' Taking an interest in selling and realising that this was an area in which, through his own efforts and with setting his goals, he could succeed, Brain Tracy had discovered a very important thing, that to go forward you have to have goals to aim at. New to the world of sales but convinced that he had a flair for it, Tracy began to read everything he could get his hands on about various selling techniques. He studied successful sales representatives and copied their winning ways. At first, he was not very successful and often did not have enough money to eat or put a roof over his head. Nevertheless, undaunted he carried on, sleeping in his car if he had to, but taking inspiration from his more successful colleagues. Gradually his results picked up and at the end of the next six-month period, he had gained the top slot in sales in his company. His goals were coming closer and the future was looking brighter.

As Brian Tracy progressed to becoming a manager, true
to form he studied everything he could about managing
people. This was a man with clear goals, which through
his hard work and study he was attaining, one by one. His
determination and strength of mind paid off and before
too long he had built a successful sales organisation with a
presence in many countries. The real estate industry was
next on his list of goals and he approached his entry into that
industry with his customary careful study of all there was
to know about buying and selling property. He talked to big
developers, learning from their experiences and, surprisingly
perhaps, took on as his first project the building and leasing
out of a three-million-dollar shopping centre.

But Tracy was not a man to rest on his laurels. He had other
goals to pursue and went back to school at night to gain
the necessary qualifications, starting with his high school
diploma. It would be easy for someone who had already
had the success he had to decide that he was beyond high
school diplomas, but that is the beauty of planning and goal
setting, if it is done properly, you will not take the short
cut, you will put in the slog and you will do well! Following
his high school diploma, Tracy eventually gained entry to
an MBA program to study business theory and marketing,
which enabled him to become a management consultant.
Tracy's study habit was a hard one to break and now he
applied it to studying how to be happy.

This is one of the goals that we all have and Tracy took
his tried and tested method towards studying this as well.
To learn about happiness, he read what he could find on
metaphysics, psychology and motivation, and when he got
married you won't be surprised to learn, I am sure that he
studied all he could about parenting. His goals were being
reached but Tracy's imagination went further than his own
life. To get a sense of perspective, and to try to understand

why some countries were rich and others poor, he added history, economics and politics to his studies.

However, that old question, the one that had started Brain Tracy off on his road to success was still there: "What makes some people more successful than others?" Tracy though he might know, his experience might have taught him and he decided to put everything he knew into a 'success system' that could help others reach their goals. He designed a seminar, which although it took about three years to really catch on eventually offered him the attainment of a further goal, and gave countless others a chance to plan for their own success, to set the goals that would make their lives the success that Brain Tracy's has been. There may be few people who have not heard of this man and his programmes that have become synonymous with success and attainment.

Brian Tracy and his hard slog, his inching towards one goal after another is a lesson to us all. Motivation is fine, determination and rising above obstacles in your way and overcoming a bad beginning are essential, your mindset is also crucial to your success, but without planning and setting goals you will be like a rudderless ship. It will be easy for you to be blown off course, even end up on the rocks. Your goals are your markers along the way, the signposts to your ultimate fulfilment. Make them carefully remember the old adage 'don't run before you can walk', make sure that you do not derail yourself before you even start by setting unattainable goals, be logical in progressing your goals towards your ultimate aim and make each goal reach the gateway to your next achievement. Do all this, and you will be the success you deserve to be.

Planning

From what you have examined already, you know the importance of having that desire to succeed, having determination and a positive mind-set. So if you have all this is it going to be plain sailing? Well it might be, but there is another important ingredient that you need if you truly want to succeed and fulfil your potential, to reach your goals and make the success out of your life that you are all capable of, which is planning.

Planning is important and is the backbone of the body of your effort. An organised approach to what you do, what you plan to do, and to everything you undertake will make your journey to your goal smoother, less likely to be snagged on avoidable hazards, delayed on stumbling blocks that could have been avoided with the right planning. The planning part is the missing link and why many people are failing today in every aspect of their life's endeavour. Success in life is not accidental, but a systematic, articulated and cultivated habits to achieve your desires. It is the result of habitual adherence to defined goals and a plan; more effort in realization of daily activities creates big success.

You cannot accidentally made good grades as a student, or accomplish your goals and all your heart's desires as a wish; you have to make a plan on how you will get there. Without plans, you cannot measure your goals and accomplishments. Planning is the road map and signpost to your desired destination. If you do not know where you are going, you cannot get there. For everything you have responsibility for in your life, you need to make clear-cut plans, do not just go through life vaguely. Make plans and preparations to achieve your dreams. In the journey of life you need to have a mission statement of how you plan to work out the bits to achieve your goals, a dream and wish alone is not enough, you need to follow it up with a defined plan.

Write down your long- term plan for what you wish to accomplish in the next five to ten years or near future and put them in front of you daily. Make your short-term plans on what you want to accomplish now, this will help you access where you are, and how well you are progressing to achieve your long-term plan.

So if you are not a naturally organised person how do you achieve the planning that is necessary to oil the wheels of the train of your success? As we have said before, the mind needs to be focused, uncluttered with trivial or inconsequential things, able to formulate and execute your plan for success. Remember that trying to achieve something that you have never done before, aspiring to be something or someone that you have not previously been means change, adaptation and belief that the person you are and that you will become is absolutely the right person to undertake your plan, fulfil your desires and deliver your ultimate goal.

You have to believe in yourself and your plan. How do you expect that anyone else will take you seriously if you doubt yourself? This is where your plan can be your best friend. Committed to paper, in black and white, it is always there so that in a weak moment, a moment of self doubt, the plan will remind you of the route you have chosen, the goals you have set and the belief that you have in yourself to attain the ultimate prize. Goals without a plan are indistinguishable, you may not know how to get there, but start from the basic steps to get your main goals and gradually you will definitely get there.

When making a plan, remember to include others that can help you when you're weak and to follow those who have accomplished much in your area. You need a mentor who can help you through. Have a plan to improve yourself, study materials in your field to help you learn more on what you want to do, and strategize to get your goals. Life will not drop success on your way... take conscious steps to make it work.

In life, I have found that successful people all have one thing in common; they learn and love to practice. They take time to sit down and create a clear blueprint (visualise the mental picture) of what they want for themselves and their future. It is time for you to make adequate plans, and to learn from the experts and those who had made it despite their social, economic and psychological background. Those who have diligently followed these basic steps have gone from rags to riches and grass to grace.

Words from great achievers

Courtesy of Brian Tracy quote.com, here are some quotes that should help you focus your mind and formulate your plan from people who have mastered the art!

You were born to win, but to be a winner, you must plan to win, prepare to win, and expect to win.

Zig Ziglar

A nation or civilization that continues to produce soft-minded men purchases its own spiritual death on the instalment plan.

Martin Luther King Jr.

Any idea, plan, or purpose may be placed in the mind through repetition of thought.

Napoleon Hill

Create a definite plan for carrying out your desire and begin at once, never wait until everything is set, whether you are ready or not, put this plan into action.

Reduce your plan to writing. The moment you complete this, you will have definitely given concrete form to the intangible desire.

Man falls from the pursuit of the ideal of plain living and high thinking the moment he wants to multiply his daily wants. Man's happiness really lies in contentment.

Mohandas Gandhi

I can only say that there is not a man living who wishes more sincerely than I do to see a plan adopted for the abolition of slavery.

George Washington

*Our goals can only be reached through a vehicle of a plan,
in which we must fervently believe, and upon which we must
vigorously act. There is no other route to success.*

Pablo Picasso

*All endeavour calls for the ability to tramp the last mile,
shape the last plan, and endure the last hour's toil. The fight
to the finish spirit is the one... characteristic we must possess
if we are to face the future as finishers.*

Henry David Thoreau

*No matter how carefully you plan your goals they will never
be more that pipe dreams unless you pursue them with gusto.*

W. Clement Stone

*If you deliberately plan on being less than you are capable of
being, then I warn you, you will probably be unhappy all the
days of your life.*

Abraham Maslow

*If you go to work on your goals, your goals will go to work on
you. If you go to work on your plan, your plan will go to work
on you. Whatever good things we build end up building us.*

Jim Rohn

If you don't design your own life plan, chances are you'll fall
into someone else's plan. And guess what they have planned
for you? Not much.

It takes as much energy to wish as it does to plan.

Eleanor Roosevelt

*The man who makes everything that leads to happiness
depend upon himself, and not upon other men, has adopted
the very best plan for living happily. This is the man of
moderation, the man of manly character and of wisdom.*

Plato

Chapter 2

*I try to learn from the past, but I plan for the future by
focusing exclusively on the present. That's where the fun is.*
Donald Trump

*A good plan violently executed now is better than a perfect
plan executed next week.*
George S Patton

*Do you wish to rise? Begin by descending. You plan a tower that
will pierce the clouds? Lay first the foundation of humility.*
Saint Augustine

So where do you start? When do you start? How can you
plan ahead when you don't know what the future holds?
Well this is the secret. Populate your plan with the salient
points of your mindset. Where your mindset, determination
and even your God-given talents will sustain and inspire
you, you still need a plan that brings together as a tangible
force your aspirations and dreams. Write it down! Many
people today have five or ten-year plans to keep them on
track, remind them of what they are working towards, and
as they reach each rung on their ladder they feel a deserved
sense of accomplishment and achievement.

However, what I want you to do is to expand that five or
ten-year plan to be a whole-of-your-life plan. Be that person
who in years to come, other people write about, the person
that is held up as a shining example, the person that had a
plan that saw them succeed where others failed, that held
fast to their plan when everything was stacked up against
them, using it to navigate through life's ups and downs.
Your mindset, your determination, your talent and your
plan are the tools you need. On the other hand, the plan is
what pulls all the different areas of your aspiration together,
which gives you a framework to build on.

A word of caution: Plans, as they say, are made to be broken. Be realistic and don't be afraid to adjust your plan if it is obvious that you need to. Alter, adapt, change if you have to but whatever it metamorphises into, make sure that you have your plan, and you know your plan. Your success depends on it!

In his book, *Flight Plan*, Brian Tracy gives us good advice. "When you are absolutely clear about who you are, what you want, and where you want to go, you will accomplish ten times as much as the average person, and much faster as well."

It is true that most of us have four main goals in common. And Brian Tracy lists these for us as:

1. Being fit and healthy and live a long life.
2. To be able to work at a job that we enjoy and to be paid well for doing it.
3. To have flourishing loving relationships with people whom we love and respect and who love and respect us as well.
4. To be financially independent and not to have to worry about money, or the lack of it ever again.

So if you take these four aims, and give yourself marks out of ten as to where you are with them, it is obvious that the aim which has the lowest points, is going to be the one that is giving the most problems. If you can concentrate on the area in which you have scored the lowest and do something about it, make a plan to get your score up, you will find marked improvement in a surprisingly short time.

Taking Tracy's flight plan analogy further, he tells you that when you are flying towards one of your desired locations you can do so with either an attitude of 'abundance' or 'scarcity'. This is where your attitude directly affects your plan. Flying forwards with an abundant attitude changes our view of the world and your own place in it and will fill you with confidence, optimism and the positive attitude you need to succeed. Changing your attitude, your perception of everything that affects you, will make you see things completely differently. The attitude that you have to the world will help you; in other words, positivism breeds completion. Approaching those same goals and taking that same flight towards our desires with a defeatist attitude or an attitude of scarcity will have the opposite effect. If you constantly blame other factors for your failure to stick to or execute your plans, you are on the road to failure. If you give yourself excuses for not undertaking this challenge or overcoming that hurdle, you will talk yourself into failing. The old 'can-do' attitude may be a bit of a cliché but it is truly the attitude that will let you achieve your plan.

When you set the goals that make up your plan, really think about those goals and how you will feel on the day that you achieve that milestone, or that achievement. Write it down, commit it to paper and to history and be definite and precise in what you are trying to achieve. Tracy urges you to be so clear and so simple about what your goals and plans are that a child could read and understand what you have written and then explain it to another child! And this is undoubtedly the secret, keep it simple, keep it clear and do not fudge those details.

Do not give yourself woolly targets and imprecise aims. Life will be tough enough on your dreams, do not start by being fuzzy, hold on tight, and focus! Close your eyes and really imagine yourself there, in that moment in your future when all your plans, hard work, discipline and determination pay off. How will you feel? Then cling to that feeling, it will be yours one day. Your plan for your life and victory, the positive seeds that you have sown for them to flourish.

Diligence

'Diligence' in the Collins English Dictionary is defined as 'careful and persevering in carrying out duties'. In other words, it is earnest and persistent application to an undertaking, steady effort, assiduity, attentive care; heedfulness.

If you look at the life of any successful person, you will always see the same pattern — their persistent application to the work that they have taken on in order to reach their set goals. A steady effort and attention to details, an understanding of what it takes to succeed and to reach their goals. Diligence is what your teacher always wished you had more of at school and it is what you need if you are to succeed. Success is not inadvertent, it is planned. Successful and powerful men and women have not achieved their success by accident, they are where they are because of their diligence, because they understood what the word meant and how taking the necessary small steps, going through the tedious slog and seemingly endless learning process would eventually deliver to them the fruits of their labours.

There are no short cuts; nothing that can replace diligence or that can be used instead to lay the groundwork for your success. Diligence is it and mastering it, learning to accept that through diligence you will progress is a powerful concept to take on board. You have heard it said that knowledge is power. Well, knowledge has to be gained, diligent process undertaken and attention to the smallest detail accepted as a given, before any success is possible. God rewards those who diligently work to attain success. There is a man whose name might be written next to that dictionary definition of diligence and that man is Anthony Robbins.

Anthony Robbins' Story

Anthony Robbins was born in north Hollywood in 1960. Like a lot of children he had to go through the divorce of his parents when he was 7 years old. Although his mother did marry she later said that her son was instrumental in driving away her husbands. "Tony would never shut up, even as a child," she said. Anthony took the name of Robbins from his first stepfather.

It was not until he was in his thirties that it was discovered that Anthony had suffered from a condition called pituitary adenoma. This disease manifests itself as an imbalance to growth hormones making them several times higher than they should be and contributing in Antony's case to his extraordinary height (6 foot 7 inches) and large hands and feet. Fortunately this tumour is benign and although Tony could have had it removed he decided not to as it was not causing him any symptoms.

Tony Robbins was a man who pursued his dreams and goals in life through diligence. His start in life and the fact that his mother blamed his garrulous ways for her marriage break-ups must have made life uncomfortable for the young Anthony. Indeed his first marriage, although it lasted 15 years, also ended in divorce. Anthony has been recorded as saying that it was the best decision of his life. The reason he gave for ending the marriage shows what a diligent person he is. He evaluated the situation and discovered that if he and his wife stayed married it would ruin both of their lives. And even more than this, he says he knew that his wife's life would be ruined more than his own.

But Anthony was not going to be a man to whom life happened. He was going to make an impact. He worked for Jim Rohn promoting his seminars, and gaining an interest in this area of motivational teaching. His diligent study of neuro-linguistics from NLP co-founder John Grinder and his subsequent inspired work in this area have made him a man to listen to, and to respect. Grinder also encouraged Anthony to have a look at the fire-walking experience. This is a total act of faith, where the participant walks in bare feet over burning coals, common in many religions as a rite of passage or a way of affirming faith and designed to show the ability to exert mind over matter. This is an area with huge potential for problems, but such is Anthony Robbins' belief in himself and so confident was he with his in-depth and diligent understanding and mastering of this technique that he introduced it to his own motivational talks and seminars. This proved to be the turning point for Anthony Robbins and the spectacle of this remarkable feat attracted the attention of the media.

Anthony Robbins conducts phenomenal motivational seminars, and writes books that certainly inspire, but it has not been easy for him. Before he became successful, Robbins lived from one pay packet to another often struggling to pay his mortgage every month. But his belief in himself as a peak performance coach and his hunger to learn all that he could in the life he was working in eventually delivered his goals to him.

Robbins has been sought out by the great and the good, including Presidents Clinton, Miterrand and Gorbachev, Margaret Hilda Thatcher, the first UK woman prime minister, and even Princess Diana. You can be sure that none of these illustrious people would have knocked on Robbins' door if they had not been utterly convinced of his strengths.

This shows us a different way in which to reach our goals, or rather an additional quality that we will need to make our lives the success that they are capable of being.

Robbins' diligence was necessary alongside his determination and his self-belief to give himself a solid basis from which to set out his stall. Do you think that anyone would have listened to him if he had not studied diligently and in depth, and understood the methods he used to teach and motivate to coach and bring out the best in people? If his work had not been backed up by solid and sustainable teaching, fact and provable concepts, he would have failed long ago. Anthony Robbins teaches us the value of diligent study and the understanding that is necessary to ensure our excellence in our field of endeavour. His area of expertise in particular requires faith from people, and that faith will not be sustained if its basis is not as solid as a rock. Robbins has been reported as saying that he prefers to be seen as a peak performance coach rather than a temporary motivator. He has studied what people do and how they behave at the peak of their ability and aims to teach them the way to access this 'peak performance' whenever they need it.

And you can be your own peak performance coach. Know what you have to learn about your specialist area and then learn it, and then learn it some more. Be diligent in your studies and always aim to be the one who knows just that bit more, the bit more that will put them ahead of others pursuing the same goals. There is no shortcut for learning, no substitute for diligent study. This is the hard graft, the building blocks that you need to make your foundations as secure as they can be.

Add careful and diligent study to your plan for your success and you will never have to worry about your empire collapsing. With knowledge behind you, you will always be able to answer your critics and justify your words and actions.

The only thing stopping you being as successful as Anthony Robbins is you!

Focus

So far, I have given you a lot of think about and a lot to aim for in your personal journey to success. The next concept that I want to talk about is focus. Sounds easy? Well it isn't and it is the lack of focus that has derailed many a promising business or venture. Focus is something you have to maintain, even when the world pushes in on you and other things vie for your attention, focus is what you need to keep you on course. Along with your goals and your diligence, your focus has to be constant and unwavering. It is easy to be distracted, to be put off or to give in to compromise when things get tough, but if you focus not only on your ultimate goal but also on the work you are doing along the way that will get you there, you will succeed. If you likened your journey to success, to building a house, where determination and mindset are the foundations, and diligence and goal setting the fabric of your building, focus is the architect overseeing all that is done and making sure that all the different parts of the project come together so that everything works towards the ultimate goal – your success.

Sir Richard Charles Nicholas Branson's Story

When a man is focused, he cannot be distracted. A man who can truly demonstrate what can be achieved by focus is Sir Richard Charles Nicholas Branson. Here are two quotes from the man who has the knack of focusing in on an idea and making it the biggest thing to hit the market, a man known worldwide for his ability to succeed at whatever he turns his hand to.

"A business has to be involving, it has to be fun, and it has to exercise your creative instincts.

I never get the accountants in before I start up a business. It's done on gut feeling, especially if I can see that they are taking the Mickey out of the consumer."

Sir Richard Charles Nicholas Branson

Sir Richard Charles Nicholas Branson was born on July 18, 1950. He started early on his entrepreneurial career publishing a student magazine at just 16 years. Education was not a priority for Branson and he did not graduate but in 1970, he and his friend Nick Powell started the now famous Virgin brand by setting up a discount record mail order business. Branson's focus meant that his record business expanded rapidly and eventually he opened a record store on London's Oxford Street.

However, Branson was not content with this; he had other prizes in his sight and in 1972 started his own recording label, Virgin Records. Such was Branson's focus that he hit upon the perfect record to put his fledgling record company on the map, *Tubular Bells,* an instrumental piece by Mike Oldfield. That stayed in the UK music charts for 247 weeks. This man was focused on his dreams. He knew what he was aiming for and how he was going to get it. From small beginnings his Virgin Records group was eventually sold to Thorn EMI for ONE BILLION DOLLARS!!

Perhaps one of the most recognised brands in the world, Sir Richard Charles Nicholas Branson's Virgin brand is attached to many different areas of enterprise. From book publishing to the music industry, from holidays to trains and planes, Branson is a shining example of how focusing on what you want, carving out a niche for yourself, knowing what you are good at and focusing on where you can go with it can realise your dreams. Branson was not from a disadvantaged background but there is no doubt that his incredible success would be extraordinary for even the most privileged executive. He focused on what he wanted and he got it! In addition, his success has brought him opportunities that many can only dream of.

Sir Richard Charles Nicholas Branson is as passionate about his personal development and life and how he lives it as he is about his business empire. Since 1985, he has been involved in the high adrenaline world of record-breaking attempts by boat and hot air balloon. He has successfully achieved distance and speed records, but his ultimate dream of being the first person to circumnavigate the world in a hot air balloon still eludes him. As you would expect, Branson makes sure that his Virgin logo is displayed prominently during every launch, or world record attempt, an excellent source of free advertising and brand placement for the Virgin Group.

Anyone who meets this remarkable man comments on how approachable he is; and how unaffected by his wealth and advantage. Nevertheless, all say that focus and determination shine from him. If you meet any very successful person, you will notice the same thing. In every aspect of their life, even in their conversation with you their focus is absolute. Another quote from Sir Richard Charles Nicholas Branson shows how grounded he is:

"Sometimes I do wake up in the mornings and feel like I've just had the most incredible dream. I've just dreamt my life."

Sir Richard Charles Nicholas Branson

There have been other awards for the man who has focused hard to achieve what he has. He was awarded a knighthood in 1999 and became Sir Richard Charles Nicholas Branson, an honour given for his contribution to entrepreneurship.

So how can you use focus on your way to the top? How can you learn it? Well there are no classes in focusing. You have to discipline yourself, be strong and uncompromising when it comes to focus. Have that picture in your mind, the one that represents where you want to be. Never be satisfied on a temporal measure, but develop your skill and keep your eyes on your journey where you will be.

Your focus will strengthen your capacity to know and acknowledge your feelings and their connection to your thinking and acting in the world, and that is what you will need each time you feel yourself in danger of slipping from your path. Your focus is a picture of your future, what you are capable of and what you wish to be, in the pursuit of your goals. It is the foundational process in strengthening of emotional intelligence. Isn't that worth making the extra effort for?

Focus gives you a practical and powerful process that guides you toward a firm emotional self-awareness, self-confidence, self-esteem and a more helpful way of living. It assists you in making the right decisions and strengthens your sense of creative ability to a winning way.

Enthusiasm

If you consider the word 'enthusiastic', what comes to mind? Is it, like for me, the picture of a puppy, full of the joy of life, eager to explore the world, and throwing himself into every new experience? Well a puppy is a good example of enthusiasm and it is something that we need if we are going to succeed. Sounds easy, doesn't it? After all, the dream you have of your success, of your ultimate goal in life is exciting and it is not difficult to feel enthusiastic about it. Well that's true, but when the first thrill of excitement passes and the hard slog begins, obstacles have to be overcome and setbacks put behind you; your enthusiasm may start to waver.

Every successful person on their way to the top has had dark days, days when, despite their best efforts, everything seems to be against them and their goals seem unattainable. It is at these moments that we need our enthusiasm for our ideal, our complete belief in our goal. With enthusiasm, we can get the energy back into our journey; we can infect others with our enthusiastic approach and pave the road to our success. Enthusiasm is your cheerleader, and it will get you where you deserve to be.

Chapter 2

Joel Osteen's Story

There can be no better example of enthusiasm and what
it can do for your life goals than Joel Osteen. This is a
man whose enthusiasm for the evangelical message was
so great that he left school without graduating so that he
could help his father in his ministry. Joel's father developed
the Lakewood church in 1959. The fledgling church soon
swelled to 6000 members with an active television ministry.
Joel's enthusiasm for the ministry shone from him and his
father recognised that his son was the one with the same
calling as he had and was the one with the enthusiasm
and dedication to join him in his ministry. Why Joel was
touched with the enthusiasm and the devotion above his
other siblings, we will never know, but it was obvious in
him from a young age. His father recognised that and
together Joel and his father made a charismatic team. The
father and son team were unstoppable, their enthusiasm for
their message unmistakable and together they developed
conferences, missionary support and also distributed food,
taking on the most taxing of tasks just as enthusiastically as
the most pleasant.

When Joel's father died in 1999, Joel was faced with big
shoes to fill. He had been very close to his father, they had
been a team and without his rock and his inspiration, Joel
was hit hard. He had always been the enthusiastic backbone
of the ministry and supported his preacher father, but in
his grief he wasn't sure that he could fill the void that his
father had left. In fact Joel had only preached once before
his father died, and that was in the week before his death
when his father listened with pride from his hospital bed to
Joel's debut as a preacher. Now Joel had to test his mettle.
Somehow he had to master his grief and focus on the
ministry, his father's memory an inspiration. And Joel found
the strength to go on, he drew on his enthusiasm and belief
in what he and his father had worked so hard for to pull him

through. He need not have worried, his natural enthusiasm made him a convincing and loved preacher, his preaching style focusing more on the goodness and loving nature of God rather than on sin.

Joel went from strength to strength and soon the Lakewood congregation needed a bigger sanctuary as they grew from about 6,000 to about 30,000 under Joel Osteen's leadership. Late in 2003, the church signed a long-term lease with the city of Houston to acquire the Compaq Centre. This former sports arena, once called The Summit, had had tenants that had included the Rockets, the Houston Aeros and the Houston Comets.

This ambitious expansion plan was not without its criticism. Joel recalled a lunch he had with city leaders when someone stated bitterly that it would be a *"cold day in hell"* before Lakewood Church was admitted to the Compaq Centre.

The church had to pay an eye-watering $11.8 million in advance rent for the first 30 years of the lease, and renovations were estimated at $95 million. On July 16, 2005, Lakewood Church moved to the newly renovated 16,800-seater centre and gained twice the capacity of its former site. There were many who thought that the arithmetic alone would doom Joel's ambitions for the expansion of Lakewood Church but Joel was steadfast in his belief and in his enthusiasm to deliver the best to his congregation.

"I guess today is a cold day in hell because Lakewood Church has now been worshipping God in the location formerly known as the Compaq Centre since July 2005," Osteen remarks in his book Become a Better You.

So what made the church grow? Osteen credits the seeds his parents planted and their faithful devotion to the task of encouraging others but there is no doubt that Joel's own enthusiasm and belief in his path played an enormous part in continuing what his parents had started. His enthusiasm gave him the belief in his mission and the ability to take on the responsibility of taking on and delivering the dreams of others, his enthusiasm took others with him, unable to resist his love of life, of God and of his congregation.

And so infectious is his enthusiasm that he is now seen in 100 countries across the world, his message and enthusiastic love of his fellow man and God is irresistible to his followers.

Currently, Joel Osteen and several Lakewood Church team members travel across the nation, presenting their programmes in large stadiums. The event, which is entitled 'A Night of Hope', includes music that is led by the church's music ministry, a moving and inspirational testimony by Joel's mother Dodie and a sermon from Joel Osteen himself.

In 2007, the tour was expanded to include appearances in several other countries, including Canada, England, Northern Ireland and Israel. Osteen released his second book, titled *Become a Better You: 7 Keys to Improving Your Life Every Day* in October 2007, and perhaps not surprisingly, it topped the New York Times Best Sellers List with a first printing of three million copies. Osteen told Larry King the new book was designed to focus more on relationships and not getting stuck in a rut where we find ourselves in life.

"That is just my basic message of becoming all God's created you to be," he added.

Osteen's popularity has led to him being featured as one of the 10 Most Fascinating People of 2006, and was named 'Most Influential Christian in America' in 2006 by *The Church Report.*

But Osteen has not been without his critics. On December 23, 2007 in an edition of the very popular *Fox News Sunday,* the programme host Chris Wallace levelled criticisms at

Osteen for his lack of Scripture reference in his sermons, as well as his apparent reluctance to discuss sin as an integral part of life. But Osteen responded: *"And I am ultimately trying to do that, but I'm trying to teach people how to live their everyday lives, and so I do focus on it, probably not as much as some people would like."* His sermons and writings are sometimes criticised for their adherence to the tenets of the prosperity church, a belief that wealth and power are rewards for pious Christians.

So how has this charismatic and successful man made his life and ministry the success it is? How has he succeeded where others have failed? Well if it were just about hard work and application, then anyone could and would succeed. But that important ingredient, enthusiasm, has to be there. Especially for Joel Osteen who has a message for his fellow man, if he is not enthusiastic about it, how would he inspire others? And how can you utilise enthusiasm to help you succeed? Well, here's how. Get in touch with your inner puppy, imagine the idea you have and the plans you have made for your success in a eureka moment; a moment of blinding realisation that you have the capability to get where you deserve to be, the moment when you see clearly ahead of you the road you need to travel, the success waiting to be achieved.

The enthusiasm you have for your aspirations should know no bounds, you have to be able to enthuse yourself before you can get others to believe in you. And if you approach even the most mundane task with the enthusiasm that you approach the most exciting, you will find it easier and easier to travel that road to your dreams. Enthusiasm will be with you through all your ups and down, it will keep your spirits up and your mind focused on the task ahead, it will make you charismatic, a person that other people want to be with, want to be involved with and those people will help you on your way. But most of all enthusiasm will keep you sane and remind you why you deserve to succeed!

Passion

If you think about passion for a cause, for self-sacrifice and
hardship endured for the absolute passion that someone has
for their life's work, many of us would think immediately
of Agnes Gonxha Bojaxhiu (Mother Theresa). However,
before we go into her life and her work let us think about
passion for a moment. Unless you believe passionately in
what you are doing, in what you have undertaken or what
you are promoting, how would you expect to convince
anyone else? Your passion for your goal in life must be
absolute; you have to believe in yourself and what you are
doing, passionately, to succeed.

It is rather like the passion that we feel at the beginning of a
love affair, that period when our heart is in our mouth each
time that person appears, when we are focused on them
and on what we are doing together, where we are going and
how we feel about our time with them. That same passion
must be with us and must be sustained as we work towards
our ultimate goal in life, our success depends on it and the
perception of us by others will be influenced by it.

Your success in business is going to be determined in a large
part by your enthusiasm. Polish that enthusiasm and passion
and show it in your dealings with others, your presentation
of yourself and your business, whatever it is, letting them
see that your passion is going to ensure their success if they
are associated with you. A successful business is made up
of many different factors and a successful businessman or
woman is also the product of many different supporting
qualities. Your passion for what you do, how you conduct
your business and where you are taking your business have to
be obvious to everyone that comes in contact with you. Have
you ever heard the expression 'Their passion was shining
out of their eyes'? Well it is as real and as tangible as that, if
you are passionate, people can see the manifestation of that
passion in your eyes, in your manner, and most importantly,
in your SUCCESS!

Agnes Gonxha Bojaxhiu (Mother Theresa)'s Story

Agnes Gonxhe Bojaxhiu was born in 1910 in Macedonia. She was the youngest in the family and her father died when she was 8 years old. From an early age, Agnes was fascinated by stories of missionaries and the passionate ministries that they undertook. By the time that she was 12 the fledgling Agnes Gonxha Bojaxhiu had decided that her passion too was going to be doing God's work. At 18 she left home to become a nun. Her first step was to study English in Ireland, as this was the language in which the children of India were taught. Her passion was finally rewarded when she arrived in India in 1929 and then took her first religious vows as a nun in 1931. It was at that time that she chose the name Teresa. She eventually took her solemn vows in 1937 while she was teaching in eastern Calcutta. Although Teresa did enjoy her teaching the poverty that she saw around her stirred a passion in her. A famine brought misery and death to the city and Hindu/Muslim violence in 1946 visited horror and despair on an already struggling city.

In September of 1946, Teresa describes hearing "the call within the call" that directed her passion for her fellow man, telling her that she should go and live amongst the poorest and the most downtrodden. So Teresa changed out of the habit that she had worn as a nun and wore instead a simple white cotton sari with a blue border. She adopted Indian citizenship and ventured into the slums. She started her mission with the establishment of a school but soon turned her attention to the starving and destitute people of the city. Although at last Teresa had found a direction for her passion, she records that the first year was very hard. Having no income she had to beg for supplies and for food. Teresa admitted to feeling very lonely in her struggle and at times a return to the comforts of convent life was tempting. She wrote the following in her diary at the time:

Our Lord wants me to be a free nun covered with the poverty of the cross. Today I learned a good lesson. The poverty of the poor must be so hard for them. While looking for a home I walked and walked till my arms and legs ached. I thought how much they must ache in body and soul, looking for a home, food and health. Then the comfort of Loreto [her former order] came to tempt me. 'You have only to say the word and all that will be yours again,' the Tempter kept on saying... Of free choice, my God, and out of love for you, I desire to remain and do whatever be your Holy will in my regard.

I did not let a single tear come.

Agnes Gonxha Bojaxhiu went on to be the founder of the Missionaries of Charity in Calcutta in 1950. Such was the passion that this tiny woman had for the poor and the poverty-stricken that she devoted her life to their care. For over 45 years she cared for the poor and the sick, orphaned children and the dying. Think about this last sentence for a moment. Forty-five years of working with abandoned children, lonely, poor, malnourished and abused people who had fallen sick in the squalor of the back streets of Calcutta. Working with people that were the dregs of society, to whom no importance was attached and to whom no other help was offered. And what kept her working with these poor people and also drove her to expand her mission to help yet more people in other countries? Her passion for her fellow man, her passion for children and for the poor who needed kindness and comfort, who otherwise would be thrown onto the scrapheap of life. Her passion expanded to embrace 610 missions in 123 countries and she was also responsible for hospices and homes of HIV/Aids sufferers, for lepers and counselling centres for families, schools and orphanages.

Agnes Gonxha Bojaxhiu's passion for her work has brought her praise from many individuals, from governments and charitable organisations. She has been awarded the Nobel peace prize and has been beatified for her passion, by the Pope. But Agnes Gonxha Bojaxhiu has also faced criticism for her stance against abortion, borne of her passion for human life and its preservation and also because she professed to believe that there was spiritual goodness in poverty. She also baptised the dying.

But no criticism, no detraction could dampen the passion of Agnes Gonxha Bojaxhiu for her fellow man. There are countless numbers of men, women and children who no-one else cared about who were literally saved to live that would not have been possible if not for Agnes Gonxha Bojaxhiu. And for you to succeed, whatever your aim or your field of endeavour you have to have the passion of Agnes Gonxha Bojaxhiu, have to be able to counter criticism, stick to your beliefs when others try to derail you, love what you are doing with all your strength and might, believe passionately and uncompromisingly in what you are doing and where you are going for this is the only veritable tool that can accelerate you faster to achieving excellence.

Discipline and strength

We all know that it is going to take discipline and strength to reach our goals in life. The greater the goal the more disciplined and the stronger we will have to be. Disciplining ourselves is an essential part of preparing ourselves for the difficult road ahead. And discipline is what we will need to stop ourselves from being distracted and succumbing to the easier path. You may often have heard it said of successful people that 'their strength of character was obvious' and that is exactly what you are going to need to ensure your success! Most roads to success involve sacrifice and that is when your disciplined approach to your life and your goal will help you the most. Rely on that discipline to keep you focused and on the right path, hold onto that strength when you encounter setbacks and obstacles, between them, these two very important assets will be your tools to ensuring your ultimate SUCCESS!

If we want to demonstrate discipline and strength of character, there are many role models we could call on, all successful people have mastered them to be where they are today, but one person who I think demonstrates these qualities admirably is Rosa Louise McCauley Parks.

Rosa Louise McCauley Parks' Story

Rosa was born in Alabama in 1913 and her maiden name was McCauley. Her heritage was colourful, her father being African American with Cherokee and Greek thrown into the mix and her mother was of Scottish Irish descent. Rosa's childhood was not an easy one; she was small for her age and suffered bad bouts of tonsillitis throughout her childhood. Her parents separated and the young Rosa moved with her mother and brother to live with her maternal grandparents in another part of Alabama. She had a strong Christian faith and started her membership of the African Methodist Episcopal Church while she grew up on her grandparents' farm. Rosa left school at 11 years of age to go to the Industrial School for Girls where she took both academic and vocational courses.

Rosa went on to study at the Alabama State Teachers College for Negroes but had to drop out to care first for her grandmother and then her mother when they became ill. At the time that Rosa was young segregation still existed and black and white people were segregated in every aspect of daily life. This included public transport where the transport companies did not supply separate accommodation for blacks and whites, but rather enforced segregated seating within their vehicles. For black children, however, there were no school buses of any type. Rosa remembers seeing the bus full of white children passing her every day as she walked to school, but accepted it as a way of life.

But this way of life, despite Rosa recalling the kindness of some white people to her, had a darker side. The Ku Klux Klan apparently marched down the street in front of her house while her grandfather guarded the door with a shot gun. For the young Rosa this must have been terrifying. Twice arsonists attacked even the college that she attended, established specifically for black people.

Rosa married a barber named Raymond Parks in 1932, a man who was active in civil rights and in campaigning for the freedom of a group of black men, the Scottsboro Boys, wrongly accused of raping two white women. Her husband recognised the strength and discipline present in his wife and with his encouragement Rosa went back to her studies and gained her high school diploma. By now she had developed a strong sense of social injustice and although it took her three attempts she was eventually registered to vote.

Rosa joined the civil rights movement in 1943 and became the only woman in the Montgomery Chapter of the NAACP (National Association for the Advancement of Coloured People) and became its secretary, because, she said, *"I was the only woman there and I was too timid to say no!"*

Then came the incident that Rosa Louise McCauley Parks is famous for and that took all the strength and discipline that she had within her. After a hard day at work at her job in a department store, Rosa got onto a bus at about 6pm. She paid and walked up to the first row of seats at the back of the bus, that were reserved for black people. Although there was a ruling that if all seats were taken those getting on later in the bus route would have to stand, bus drivers had taken it upon themselves to get black people to give up their seats if the white seating was full up. And this is what the bus driver now did, asking Rosa and four others to give up their seats to create another 'whites only' row. Rosa recalled what happened next: *"When that white driver stepped back toward us, when he waved his hand and ordered us up and out of our seats, I felt a determination cover my body like a quilt on a winter's night. The driver wanted us to stand up, the four of us. We didn't move at the beginning, but he says 'Let me have those seats' and the other three people moved but I didn't."*

The police were called and Rosa was arrested. But her stand sowed a seed for the freedom that black Americans enjoy today, and her discipline, her strength and her belief in her cause are something that we all need to emulate if we are to bring the same strength to our journey to success.

There are many stories of bravery of sacrifice to a cause that we could cite, but this quiet and unassuming young woman can teach us a lot in our own endeavours. She was not loud, aggressive, abusive, rude or hostile. She did not need to be. Her disciplined approach to her life and to her dealings with the oppression she faced gained her respect and helped her cause immeasurably. She had the strength to stand up for what she believed in, and if you want to succeed, you must too!

Wisdom and Knowledge

The quality of wisdom is a hard quality to define. Knowledge is easier to understand, we can and must equip ourselves with knowledge if we are to succeed.

But wisdom — that is something different and it is a quality that sets those who are born to lead apart from everyone else. No one will admire an unwise or impetuous leader and whatever your destination in life, whatever your goal and your dream, the greatest thing that you can aspire to is to be considered wise by those who trust and do business with you. No one will trust the word of a man or woman who is unwise, but the wisdom of a learned man is always sought after. In addition, no wisdom is possible without knowledge. Surely, the greatest gift that you can give yourself is knowledge. Learning and acquiring knowledge will be the foundations of your life and what you achieve and wisdom will follow.

A man with knowledge and wisdom develops self-conscientiousness in paying proper attention to a task; giving the degree of care required in a given situation, working hard with enthusiasm and care in all actions. Great men of wisdom do everything energetically and whole-heartedly without complaint; they persevere and strive to the very end of a certain task. They persist in something even if there are any obstructions to hold down and hamper them. Men of wisdom and knowledge apply steady effort; assiduity, attentive care, and heedfulness. They realize that they have potential and diligently develop a long vision of where they are going.

Dr. Goodluck Ebele Jonathan's Story

One man who had both of these qualities in abundance and who is now at the height of his achievement is Dr. Goodluck Ebele Jonathan, the President of Nigeria.

Young Dr. Goodluck Ebele Jonathan was identified as a child destined for great things from an early age, such were the unusual qualities and attributes that he demonstrated even as a very young child.

At school Goodluck showed an early promise and was appointed Class Prefect in 1973, and so suited was he to this office that he held many offices as a schoolboy. It is rare for such a young man to be so widely admired by his peers that they unanimously vote for him to lead them, but Goodluck had qualities that others could not deny.

Dr. Goodluck Ebele Jonathan had an enduring thirst for knowledge and gained a B.Sc. (Hons.) Second Class (Upper Division). And this young man did not forget his duty to his country and served as a Corpsman, between 1981 and 1982, taking the role of classroom teacher in Community Secondary School Iresi – Oyo State (now Osun State). As a teacher, his excellent leadership qualities ensured that he was loved by all his pupils, inspiring them to do their very best.

This is a man who epitomized the phrase, 'leading by example' and his many virtues and personal integrity made him a role model whose influence no doubt inspired the many young people that he taught.

Dr. Goodluck Ebele Jonathan's career went from strength to strength with many more awards and accolades to follow. One of his abiding passions was environmental matters in which he has a passionate interest and for which he has been widely applauded. His thirst for knowledge in humanitarian studies and the environment have contributed

to the wisdom that has made him the man he is today.
It was perhaps inevitable that a man with the qualities
exhibited by Dr. Goodluck Ebele Jonathan should be called
to politics as his determination to do the best he could and
to excel at everything he did made the success of anything
he did non-negotiable. His deep interest in socio-economic
reform led him to be determined to make a difference from
within and he has been dedicated to this cause for most of
his adult life. This is not an easy road to follow and it is only
with knowledge and wisdom that any man could ever hope
to make a difference and Dr. Goodluck Ebele Jonathan was
determined that he would be that man.

Dr. Goodluck Ebele Jonathan brought stability to turbulent
political life and managed to turn people away from extreme
violence and chaos. Jonathan doggedly pursued politics
without rancour, violence or bitterness; this has made Ogbia
one of the most violence-free clans in Nigeria today. There
is little doubt that the virtues and attributes of Dr. Goodluck
Ebele Jonathan have made this possible, as his wisdom,
patience and determination guide his heart and his thinking.

Moreover, Dr. Goodluck Ebele Jonathan has been blessed in
his private life too. He is happily married to Mrs. Patience
Faka Jonathan and the couple have two children.

There is no denying the achievements of a man who
has taken on every challenge in life and through it all,
maintained his steadfast belief in making a difference
to all his countrymen. He has not shirked from his
responsibilities both to his country and to the world in
which he represents his country. He has equipped himself
to lead with knowledge and has developed a wisdom that
is respected by millions. His guidance and wisdom have
brought him to the position of President of Nigeria and his
great personal integrity and understanding of his fellow
man will ensure that he will be remembered forever as a
great leader of his country.

Like Dr. Goodluck Ebele Jonathan you will have to build the knowledge that will offer you the best hope of the future and the achievement that you want and deserve. There is no doubt that leaders like Dr. Jonathan are few and far between and represent the best chance of success for the future of their countries. Dr. Goodluck Ebele Jonathan's calm and assured hand on the future of Nigeria is a very bright and promising indication for the future of the country and its population. What is more, your best and sure hope for your future is the wisdom to choose the right path in life, to build on the knowledge that has been your foundation stone. If you can do this, you will MAKE IT.

Humility

There is no doubt that for us to succeed in life we need many qualities. The obvious ones like courage and determination we could all imagine are part of what we need to succeed but there are other less obvious qualities that are just as important. Humility is a quality that all of us should have and many of us let slip away from us as we climb the ladder of success. After all, why do we need to be humble, we are on top of our game, getting to where we want to be, that is a cause of pride not humility, surely? Of course it is important to be proud of our achievements and the hard work we have put into reaching our goals, but humility is important too. We have all heard the old saying 'pride goes before a fall', well humility keeps us grounded, makes us realise that we can fail as easily as we can succeed. Without humility, we can lose sight of the fundamentals, and we can lose touch with reality. After all, however great our own efforts have been, we would not be where we are without the input of others and the love and support of those around us.

Pastor Enoch Adejare Adeboye's Story

One man whose life is a testament to humility is Pastor Enoch Adejare Adeboye who went without shoes for the first 17 years of his life. Born on March 2, 1942 at Ifewara in Osun state to the family of Mr and Mrs Moses Adeboye, young Enoch grew up with very few of the material things of life. His family was so poor that they struggled to send him to school. Enoch's family were so poor that he recalls that there was a major celebration when they managed to save up and buy an umbrella. For the first 17 years of his life, his family were so short of money that Enoch never even had a pair of shoes.

His parents were determined that Enoch would have an education even though it was a huge struggle. But his parents put their faith in God and with His help and the assistance of his mother, Mrs Easther Adeboye, Enoch completed his education, graduating at the age of 25 in 1967. The fact that this young boy was being given the education that he needed although his parents had to make many sacrifices to allow him to study, was not wasted on young Enoch who, from the first day at primary school to his graduation from University, excelled as a humbly dedicated student, always achieving 'A' grades. He truly adhered to the ideal that what his parents lacked in material he would make up for in academic excellence.

With an M.SC in Hydrodynamics and a PhD in applied Mathematics, this softly spoken pastor began a teaching career, which went from grammar school, to an eventual career in University lecturing at the University of Ilorin and later University of Lagos. His dream then was to become the youngest Vice-Chancellor in Africa, but life had another calling for him.

Enoch's life began to change when he was invited by his uncle, Reverend Chris Fajemirokun to The Redeemed Christian Church of God to seek solution to a particular problem. As the service got underway, Dr Enoch felt the presence of God in the congregation and heard the message that if one will not change from sinful ways that person will end up in hell on the day of judgement. Enoch wasted no time in giving his life to Jesus. This was truly a momentous time for Enoch and he knew that he had to change his life so that he could be an example and an inspiration to others.

He became a born-again Christian on July 29th 1973 and in his humility acknowledged God in everything he did. He was baptised by immersion in September 1973 and as a dedicated worker in the church, he laboured to preach the Gospel of Jesus Christ through his words and deeds. Such was his desire to spread God's word that he also conducted lunch hour fellowship to the University community. Enoch was ordained a pastor of the church on September 14, 1975 and later became the official English language interpreter of Reverend Josiah Olufemi, whose message had been only in the Yoruba language. He diligently served in different departments in the church without complaint and succeeded Reverend Akindayomi when he was ordained General overseer of the Redeemed Christian Church of God in 1981.

At the age of 38, Pastor Enoch became the leader of the church, a move that surprised many of the church elders. But Pastor Adeboye has gone on to change the face of Christianity in Nigeria, Africa and the rest of the world. Unlike most preachers, his messages are centred on holiness and purity born of his own humility for which he is widely respected.

Pastor Enoch Adeboye has gone from strength to strength and the influence of this humble man and his progress in life have been captured in a blog that he writes for 'Nigerian Million Makers.'

'Nigerian Million Makers' are men and women born naked like you and me. They are men and women who face life's challenges just like every other person. The difference is that, they find solutions to such challenges. They are men and women who discover their purpose on earth and pursue it with everything they've got.

They have great passion for their calling to making life better for others. This is also true of the Nigerian Million Maker of today. The famous Billy Graham once said. *"You don't have to put greatness on to people; you just have to elicit it, for the greatness is already there".* This is certainly true of Dr. Enoch Adeboye. This great man has, through his quiet determination, his humility and hard work become a success that is not only his own but is also God's work channelled through him to reach millions of people. His humility and self-sacrifice has been rewarded. The boy who once went without shoes, can afford anything money can buy and recently bought a private jet for the promotion of the gospel of Jesus Christ.

Wherever he goes and however he travels on his quest to spread God's word, Dr. Enoch Adeboye can be proud of the hard work and determination that have given him the reward of his success. But it is his humility and it will also be your humility that will keep you grounded and in touch with the path you have trodden, that will allow you to remember the hard slog that has delivered you to your eventual SUCCESS.

Chapter 3

Step out of your comfort zone and face your future

Desire

There is no doubt that on your way to the top you are going to have to step out of your comfort zone. "Yes, yes," I hear you say, "that's obvious," but just let's just take some time to appreciate what it is really going to mean to you and your life as you know it. Therefore, you have had your idea, or your driving passion and you've set your goals, and you have your diligence and determination, your focus and your enthusiasm. Surely, it is all going to go fine. Well maybe, hopefully, but at some stage you are going to have to step outside your comfort zone, take a risk, and put your conviction to the test to fulfil your heart's desire. This is a time at which many fledgling businesses fail; sometimes because of lack of preparation, sometimes because of unrealistic expectations, and sometimes just because in the full glare of the reality spotlight, nerve is lost or conviction wavers.

This does not have to happen to you. Preparation is everything here. It may be that you have a 9-5 job and are preparing to leave the comfort of being a company paid worker to strike out on your own. Jump too soon and without adequate preparation and you could doom your enterprise to failure before it has even begun. Taking the step away from that paid sick leave and holidays, company pension and all the perks that come with being an employee is not to be taken lightly. It is a safe life; letting someone else worry about tax returns, pay on bank holidays, provision of premises and all the things that will now be your responsibility. Once you are out on your own, there will be no safety net. Before you take this step you need to know that you are able to sustain yourself and your family and any commitments you might have, like a mortgage. This is where the balancing act comes in. It is easy to be frightened off by the thought of having to 'go it alone'. It's frightening to imagine how many businesses or brilliant ideas have never seen the light of day because someone could not take that final step out of their comfort zone, could not take that ultimate risk for what they believed in.

Stuart Sharp's Story

Take the story of Stuart Sharp. This man at the age of 67, a self-trained musician, has been hailed as a genius after writing a symphony.

Stuart's revelation of the symphony that he eventually wrote came to him 35 years ago when his baby son Ben died. Stuart says that at that desperately sad time and in his grief at the death of his baby, he had a vision of the musical masterpiece that he eventually wrote. But as he stepped out of his comfort zone to try and pursue his dream he lost his marriage and all his money and ended up sleeping on the street. The fact that he could neither read music nor play any instrument did not deter him and he says that the tunes were so vivid in his mind that he was determined to find a way to produce his symphony. He said, speaking to the Mail Online about the music that haunted him for 35 years.

"My son Ben died after medical complications at birth and my wife was very ill in hospital. I was in so much trauma you cannot imagine.

Then on the night of Ben's funeral I had a vision of soothing, beautiful music and it gave me great comfort.

I could see the whole orchestra playing and as I watched I could see all the individual notes being played on the different instruments.

After that I would often hear the music and I could remember it all very vividly.

The tunes were always very real, very beautiful, sometimes as if the angels were really playing to me.

I did not know what the notes were and at times I doubted my sanity, especially as I am an atheist.

But I came to understand that it was music for my son and I could see it on stage one day."

And Stuart's persistence did eventually pay off. The London Philharmonic Orchestra has now recorded the 40-minute masterpiece and the Angeli Symphony is to be played in London's Royal Albert Hall. Music experts have hailed the symphony as a work of genius. Alan Wilson, the conductor of the London Philharmonic Orchestra had this to say about Stuart's work:

"Stuart's vision for his musical work was remarkable and it's quite astounding, that a non-professional musician has come up with something of this quality,"

"I guess it's a bit like someone attempting brain surgery without ever going to medical school — genius."

Stuart's story started conventionally enough. He married his childhood sweetheart Jo and they had a daughter, Emma in 1974. But the death of his son Ben wrenched the family apart. Jo was in hospital for over a year following Ben's death and Stuart was left to care for Emma alone. At that time Stuart was working in a pub as a chef and did his best to keep everything going while Jo was away. When Jo eventually came home from hospital the couple adopted a little girl called Kate.

But despite the fact that things seemed, at last, to be getting back to normal and Stuart could have lived a comfortable life with Jo and his daughters, he just could not settle. He started to drink heavily, up to a bottle of whiskey each night, and he had to admit to himself that if he continued, he would die. He was unhappy, depressed and he knew that the situation could not continue as it was.

Therefore, Stuart took his courage in his hands and told his wife that he wanted to write a musical work for orchestra. Given that he had no musical skills, could not read or even play a note, his wife could be forgiven for thinking that he had gone completely mad, and she told him as much. She advised her husband to get therapy, but despite the disruption to his family life, Stuart knew that this was something he just had to do. Imagine the moment that this man made the decision to leave his wife, and their children, an extreme example I know, but it shows just how far a human being is prepared to step away from everything that they hold dear, everything that is a comfort to them, to pursue their dream.

Leaving the comfortable world of family and security behind him, Stuart lived on the streets for 10 years totally convinced that he had to write his symphony. During his times on the streets Stuart took the odd causal job and lived off eating scraps, food that other people threw away. For a man used to a comfortable home and the love of his family it must have been a very shocking initiation to life on the streets. His weight dropped to 8 stone and we can only imagine the hurt and betrayal that his family felt. During this time Stuart bought a guitar for 50p and used it to give expression to the tunes that were constantly going around in his head. It seemed as though Stuart's dream was as elusive as ever until one night when he was sleeping rough outside the BBC centre in London, he met Anthony Wade, a jazz musician. What Wade saw in this down-and-out is not clear, but he gave Stuart a place to stay and helped him to transcribe the music that had been in his head for such a long time. And that might have been the end of the story, but it wasn't. Stuart got involved in sales and property and eventually became a self-made millionaire. But the symphony still had not been written and for the second time in his life Stuart decided that he had to do something about it.

"By 1994 I was rich and had a huge home in central London and I decided to buy a recording studio so I could finally realise my dream," he said.

"I tracked down Anthony and he couldn't believe how much I had achieved.

It took many years to get the tunes out of my head, but I managed it and since then I have written 30 more pieces," said Stuart.

It took Stuart several years to finally write the symphony, but it will now be a soundtrack for a documentary film, that is currently being filmed about his life story.

Stuart remembers that:

"The Philharmonia Orchestra gave a standing ovation after they played it, but it still feels strange to think I wrote it. I think after Ben died I died and became a different person."

Stuart's story is an extreme example of what can happen when a person's passion for what they want to do is so strong that they are prepared not only to leave their comfort zone but to suffer greatly because they believe in what they have to do. And Stuart is also proof that it is possible to come back from the depths of despair and make a success of your life. In Stuart's case he succeeded in business and also in his musical aspirations. His dream never left him but he recognised when the time was right to realise it, when it would be practical to do that and when he had the right support.

As you prepare to leave your comfort zone make sure that your plans are in place and that contingencies exist against anything that might go wrong.

In your calculations must be the people that depend on you for their support, and even the roof over their heads. It is true that many relationships do not survive the start of a new business and the sacrifice that that inevitably involves; so don't let your relationship be one of them! Leaving the comfort zone need not be as scary as you think if you prepare for your success and try to anticipate problems before they arise.

Communication is vital as you take that first step, especially your communication with those affected by your progress towards your dreams and aspirations. To make the transition from your comfort zone you need to have a clear idea of what you are aiming for and of anything that might upset the apple cart on the way to your dreams. Contingency plans are vital and the more preparation you undertake the calmer you will feel and the more confident. Those around you will also be comforted by your diligence and be more likely to offer wholehearted support.

This may be the biggest step you take in your life but you won't get to the realisation of your dreams without it. At some point every successful man or woman has had to take that step, that leap of faith. There is no empire or true success story that has ever been attained by someone directing the show from his or her armchair! You have to get out there, believe in yourself and be prepared to weather any storms that may disrupt your journey to success. Make sure that you have covered all the bases, don't leave things to chance, make sure that you know exactly what is going on and when it is happening within your organisation. Surround yourself with people who have the same drive and enthusiasm as you do. Get rid of any negative forces, or people who want to tell you that it can't be done, that you're punching above your weight, you don't need them or their negativity! Leaving the comfort zone can be frightening and daunting and may cause you sleepless nights, but as those doubts crowd in on you keep your aims and dreams clear in your mind, sweep away all the other negative thoughts and set your course straight for your SUCCESS!

Patricia Orlunwo Ikiriko's Story

So now, to show you that my life has been anything but straightforward, I think I should tell you a little about my own story. My life has been fulfilling but at the same time very challenging. I believe that my own story could act as an inspiration and even become a springboard to those settling for mediocrity because of their reluctance to step out of their comfort zone. Possibly children from an affluent background, wives of very rich husbands or people who are related or associated in one way or another to wealth, who have never really had to push hard for anything and for whom life, and all its riches, has always been served up on a plate.

I could be considered to be from this kind of background in some ways, but the difference is that I made a massive leap out of my comfort zone in a move that, at the time, many people thought was madness. I was born into a home with very strong family values and a close family bond and had a very comfortable childhood in Nigeria. Growing up was easy with all that makes for comfort and a good life, free of worry about money.

My childhood and that of my siblings was privileged and as these things often go, perhaps inevitably, my eldest sister and her very rich and caring husband took over the responsibility of the family at a very early stage.

Our family had a strong Christian faith and I was blessed with a loving and secure childhood that many would envy. As the third of nine children I cannot say that I stood out as an 'A' student but I did realize early on that what I wanted to become in life could best be achieved through education. I graduated with a Bachelors degree in Education in Guidance and Counselling in 1994. I went on to complete my Masters degree again in Guidance and Counselling. While in education, I lacked nothing, drove to school in the best cars, was exposed to several businesses and eventually managed a Multimillion Naira business owned by my elder sister.

I got married and had a family of my own. As a couple, we were both young and ambitious. My husband, Hope, and I were happily married and blessed with two beautiful children, Chanan-Christie Mikabuachi Ikiriko and Doxa Chiudushime Ikiriko, and two foster children, Naomi Miriam and Timiadedike Sieker, who are both now married.

I discovered I had a flair for business and started managing the family business and soon became the managing director of a leading haulage and sales company in Nigeria. On a daily basis I was involved in the decision-making process, ensuring the vision and values of the company from 1999-2007.

After each day's work I would return home to my loving husband and children. My life seemed almost perfect as we had one of the happiest homes on earth. I enjoyed the love, care and companionship of all the members of my close-knit family.

As a trained counsellor, I had worked with different organizations involved with young people, assisting those struggling with drug taking, emotional problems and frustration leading to juvenile delinquency. I was also involved in mediating and restoring broken engagements and family relationships amongst young people.

Between 2000-2006, I was actively involved with the Legislators Wives Association (LEWA) in my State, where I was able to make meaningful contributions to many public hearings. I also participated in awareness campaigns for rural dwellers' sensitization, providing survival techniques through counselling for youths involved in drug addiction, and those living with HIV and other terminal diseases.

Raising the children was a joy rather than a struggle as I enjoyed the unwavering support of my husband and our girls who were selfless in their devotion to the family. As a family we did very well, had a very successful family business and sent all the children to very good schools. They reciprocated with excellent academic effort and achievement. There is no doubt that our success was enhanced by the commitment of the domestic staff that we were blessed with. Every member of the family had the opportunity to pursue his or her career because everyone, including the domestic staff, worked as a team. My husband had his driver, and I had mine, the grown-up girls both had their personal cars. We had a housekeeper, a Nanny, a cook and a security man. Life was rewarding and enjoyable which gave us the freedom to pursue our individual careers with ease and passion, free from worry about domestic concerns. The blessing of the African extended family culture meant we never lacked love and attention, particularly from brothers and sisters.

I had always thought that my fulfilment in life would come from helping others. I believe in problem solving, establishing goals and developing a possibility-thinking attitude to ensure success in life. When faced with problems, I never quit but keep on striving for solutions.

My inspiration for helping young people was developed from watching many young people I had contact with in my profession go through life with no vision or goals, often ending up in the criminal underworld, or as juvenile delinquents.

I vowed to do something to help these young people take charge of their lives and learn how to develop the right mindset, possibility thinking, cultivation of habits, and development of a proper action plan, which would help them attain greatness. I aimed one day to write a book that could help them through life and help them accomplish their goals. I truly believe that the book will deliver my ideas and positive and enabling information to many young people to show them that no matter where they are starting from, they can attain success. But, I thought, the only way to reach my goal was to acquire the right knowledge on how to write a good book.

As my desire to help young people grew I decided that, despite the comfortable and familiar life I enjoyed with a loving family and friends in my country and the secure future that our business offered us all, I would have to pursue my studies overseas to be better equipped to fulfil my desire by exposure to other challenging environments, different values and cultural backgrounds. I needed the chance to enhance and broaden my capability to handle cases with diverse backgrounds. I wanted to equip myself with the highest qualifications and to produce a work that would offer real inspiration and guidance, and make a real difference to the lives of young people. Hence, I am presently studying for a Ph. D in Psychology at the University of Bedfordshire in the United Kingdom: my thesis is on the effects of study habits counselling on locus of control among African Senior Secondary School Students in Nigeria.

The actualization of this vision has not been easy on this new and unfamiliar path far from the familiarity of my comfort zone. It was a strange and often frustrating journey. It started with my application for admission for a professional doctorate (DPsych) in the counselling psychology programme in the University of East London where I was faced with a challenge as I was offered admission for a one-year conversion programme instead of the doctorate degree which I originally applied for. I almost rejected the offer, as I was so discouraged. And there was the weather too, I struggled to adjust and acclimatize to the extreme difference from a typical tropical climate to the harsh winter climate of England, (even though one has been a regular visitor to the UK). The thought of coming to settle down in a place with such a contrasting culture and environment was almost overwhelming.

I came to the UK with my two younger children, Doxa, who was then nine-years-old and Chanan-Christie, who had just turned six, and who were also faced with the difficulties of adjusting to the new environment and particularly struggled with the conservative nature of the European environment. Naomi had started her MSc Programme at the University of Sunderland and I had to get the children settled before I could get started with my programme and I had to do it all alone. At this time our other daughter, Timi, was living with her husband in Swaziland, which is unlike Nigeria where almost everything was at ones beck and call. In London, the routine of running from one train station to another, moving around without any personal assistant or even a car and managing in a system in which ones personality is overlooked in favour of bureaucracy was very hard.

However, the drive to overcome these problems and the commitment to become great and complete my personal and academic development in order to be more equipped to pursue my vision in life, kept me going. The challenge continued without an end in sight but even on my darkest days my confidence and consolation was that I was gaining tremendous and invaluable experience that I would not have found in my comfort zone, and that money could not buy.

Another experience that proved extremely difficult was finding a house to rent. It was a difficult experience as we discovered that majority of the accommodation was just far too small.

We had concentrated our search around East London, an area close to the University of East London where I had gained admission. We finally settled for a house in Canning town in East London. The whole of the two-bed house was not even as big as my daughter's bedroom back home but the children and I had to accept this condition as a reality we must live with, and although very uncomfortable, we did not allow it to distract us.

I am so grateful to God for the nature of the children we have, even though they were uncomfortable with the situation, they were understanding, contented and trusting, working hard at school and supporting me in any way they could.

From time to time, I was faced with the difficulties of consoling the children in their new environment, explaining our situation to them so that they would understand that it was temporary and that sacrifices had to be made for greatness to be achieved. At this time our goddaughter, Ada Elem, a diligent and precious gift from God to our family, managed the business back home and all our employees.

We settled down and we began to pursue our vision. I had been away from academic work for a few years in pursuit of business and to make ends meet and I knew that returning to academia was going to be a challenge. This made me more determined to put in the extra effort necessary to cope with my studies in an entirely different academic environment.

I never gave up and continued to push and press on, at this point I had put behind me the luxury and comfort of my former life in order to condition my mindset properly to be able to overcome the challenge before me, so that I could emerge successfully at the end of the day. As I continued, things became easier and I began to adjust to my new life. I was able to concentrate on my work, improve on my information technology skills, helping the children with their schoolwork whenever they came home from boarding school. Originally it took me about 12 hours to get the children to their boarding school and back for half terms and holidays, so immediately after my programme in the University of East London I decided I wanted to relocate closer to the children's school while I waited for my result.

Then my results came in and I had made it! I began another phase of the journey to realize my dream of studying for a professional Doctorate in Counselling Psychology. This phase again presented so many challenges that it almost destroyed my self-confidence, my hopes and dreams, and one by one, different universities rejected 12 applications. I have always believed that with God everything is possible and I kept the faith. I saw every rejection as a step to the next level to my destiny. Then, when I had almost lost hope of studying for my PhD in a UK University my husband visited us and was so concerned about the situation that he stayed up night after night searching the internet to look for alternative schools. Finally, he found the University of Bedfordshire and encouraged me to apply again. With such an encouraging husband and family, I could not give up. And finally, after all the rejections, I had an offer to study for a research PhD degree in Counselling Psychology at the University of Bedfordshire.

When I thought about all the stress of living and moving around in London, I decided it would pay to get a car to address the challenge of school runs and to generally help with our lives. It was time to get my driver's license in the UK. After acquiring my learner's permit I subsequently passed my theory test. I quickly started lessons for the practical test to qualify for a driver's license. Four failures to pass the test came at the same time that I was experiencing the rejections in my application for my study for PhD. The failures and rejections became so frequent that I could not bring myself to tell my husband the time of my driving test because I could not bear to report another failure. I was determined to work for success. I knew that this tough time would pass; I would take charge again and never surrender to failure. Although at times I felt my world was collapsing, one thing I could not accept was failure. I kept on trying and finally passed my practical driving test, at the fifth time of asking, and I was back on track on my journey to fulfilment.

The feeling of success is a feeling directly opposite to that of failure and a marvellous contrast to it. Failure is demeaning, demoralising and devastating but only those who accept it as the end of a process end up as casualties of it. If you see failures as a stepping-stone, only then will you be guaranteed success in life. There is no successful man that has not experienced failure. Failure is just an indication of the wrong way to success.

Thomas Edison said that the 500 tests he did which failed to produce electricity represented the 500 ways of how not to get it right that he learnt in the process.

I have moved on with my pursuit of fulfilment and in the process have lost touch with all the comfort and luxury I left at home in pursuit of my career.

Do I miss my family, my friends, my home and my children?

Of course I do, but I have a dream, set goals and a plan. For the success of that plan, I have to leave my comfort zone and am prepared to do whatever it takes to get me to the level I know I need to be at, where my work can make a real difference. If you want to succeed, you will have to be prepared to leave your comfort zone too. For I believe that success is not accidental, but based on adequate cultivation of habits, properly worked-out set goals, plans and diligence adherence to action plans. It may be for a short time or it may be for a long period and you may feel sad, discomforted, disconnected and at most times frustrated and may miss your comforts and routine terribly. All I can say is if you keep your eyes on the prize you have promised yourself, it will be bearable and it will be possible and you will thrive!

Chapter 4

Hold the Dream

Inspiration

However far that you have got with your journey to success, however much you have put into it and however much you have sacrificed for it, there is another essential part of the equation that you cannot ignore. You have to hold onto your dream, maintain your vision of what you are aiming for, of what you can and will achieve. Sounds easy? Well maybe, but oftentimes, the straightforward path to your success that you envisioned can become a winding and perilous road and without a firm grip on your dreams, you are in danger of running off that road and into the wilderness. Even the most carefully thought out plans and the most assiduously laid down guidelines can suffer from outside pressures and unexpected problems.

Michael Joseph Jackson's Story

One man who held his dream, even when it seemed the
world was against him is Michael Joseph Jackson. This
man, who had been a star almost from the time he could
walk, had many obstacles to overcome in his life, a life that
ended all too soon. The stories of his childhood and the
harsh and stern treatment meted out to him by his father
are well documented. It seems that Joe Jackson was the
ultimate in pushy parents. He worked all his sons hard but
it seems that, recognising the potential in Michael to be a
world phenomenon, he worked the young boy even harder.
There is a well-documented story of Joe Jackson holding his
young son upside down and beating him mercilessly on his
buttocks and lower back. Many may say that it was this
early dysfunctional childhood that made Michael Joseph
Jackson the man he was, a man riddled with self-doubt,
slavishly concerned with his appearance, under suspicion
for his dealings with children, and his behaviour with his
own children. Any number of problems beset the star
who in his lifetime was one of the most successful musical
talents of all time.

His early career was meteoric, his dance moves,
inspirational and addictive musical style won him fans all
over the world, but by the mid 1980s speculation about his
appearance started to dog Michael. His skin, which had
been a mid-brown colour, was beginning to lighten. The
media pounced upon this change, and thousands of column
inches were devoted to speculation as to how and why he
was lightening his skin. The official word was that Michael
had vitiligo, a skin condition that causes the skin to lose
colour. He also apparently suffered from Lupus although
this was said to be in remission. Both these illnesses come
with sensitivity to sunlight and it was claimed that the
creams he used for the vitiligo further lightened his skin.

For his public appearances Michael had to wear pancake makeup to even out the blotchy nature caused by the alteration in his skin pigment. The change of shape of his facial features also became a matter of much fascination for the press.

For Michael, who always cared what his fans thought, the criticism and accusations that he was somehow trying to be un-black must have hurt very deeply.

Accusations that he had anorexia nervosa also dogged the singer who lost a lot of weight in order to achieve a 'dancer's body'. Speculation went further to suggest that he had 'body dysmorphia', a psychological disorder in which the sufferer dislikes how they look and cannot see themselves as others see them. Although Michael had initially seen the publicity that surrounded him as a good thing he became increasingly saddened and frustrated by the lies and fanciful stories that were published about him and once said:

"Why not just tell people I'm an alien from Mars. Tell them I eat live chickens and do a voodoo dance at midnight. They'll believe anything you say, because you're a reporter. But if I, Michael Joseph Jackson, were to say, 'I'm an alien from Mars and I eat live chickens and do a voodoo dance at midnight', people would say, 'Oh, man, that Michael Joseph Jackson is nuts. He's cracked up. You can't believe a damn word that comes out of his mouth.'

This fascination with his personal appearance haunted

Michael throughout his life but did not put him off his dream. His dance routines and his music inspired many across the world and his loyal fans were devoted to him. He valued their support and their love and the confidence they gave him to hold onto the dream that he had suffered so much to achieve. He wrote his first autobiography in 1988, entitled *Moon Walk*. The book laid bare his abusive childhood and admitted to two surgeries on his nose.

Michael brought the famous Neverland ranch in 1988 and fulfilled another dream, maybe to compensate for a childhood spent on the road. He installed Ferris Wheels, other fairground rides, a movie theatre and a menagerie of animals; it was every child's dream backyard, filled with all the things that Michael himself missed out on when he was a boy.

In 1992, Michael founded the Heal the World Foundation. The Foundation offered under-privileged children the chance to join Michael at Neverland and enjoy a truly magical time on the rides that were dotted all over the property. Under Michael's guidance the Foundation spent millions of dollars to help children all over the world who had suffered from the effects of disease, poverty and war. Between the months of June and November 1993 Michael toured with his Dangerous World Tour that in 67 concerts played to 3.5 million people. The entire proceeds of the tour went to the Heal the World Foundation raising millions of dollars for the fund. Michael was riding high, fulfilling another dream to help children that he cared so much about, even pleading with then US President Bill Clinton in public to spend more money for relief with children infected with HIV/AIDS.

In Africa the hunger for this talented man was insatiable. Michael visited Gabon on the first stop of a tour of Africa to be greeted with a large crowd and a raucous reception with over 100,000 people there to greet him holding up signs that read 'Welcome home Michael'. When he visited the Ivory Coast he was crowned a King; King Sami by a tribal chief and had to sign formal documents that confirmed his Kingship. He was seated on a golden throne for ceremonial dances and thanked his hosts in English and then in French.

But in 1993, the wind began to change for Michael. Giving a 90-minute interview to chat show host Oprah Winfrey (only his second such interview since 1979) he looked pained as he spoke of his childhood and the realisation of how much he missed out on in his formative years, admitting that he had often cried out of loneliness. In the same interview Michael took the chance to lay to rest some of the rumours that had beset him. He completely denied the rumours that he had bought the bones of John Merrick, The Elephant Man and also poured cold water on the rumour that he bleached his skin or slept in an hyperbaric oxygen chamber. For the first time he admitted publicly that he had vitiligo. Such was the fascination with Michael Joseph Jackson that no less than 90 million people tuned in to see the interview which made it the fourth most popular non-sport programme ever in the history of US broadcasting. Importantly, and as Michael had hoped, it raised awareness of vitiligo, a condition that most people knew very little about.

But Michael's world was about to be shattered, his dream in danger of evaporating. In the summer of 1993 came the shattering accusation of child sexual abuse, levelled at Michael by a 13-year-old boy, Jordan Chandler, and his father Evan who was a dentist. Michael had known the boy for a year when Evan administered a drug called sodium amytal to his son, and he claims that under its effects (it is often called the truth drug) the boy accused Michael of touching him inappropriately. Michael was saddened and appalled by the accusation and the money that was being demanded. The Chandlers were determined to win and in a recorded telephone conversation Evan Chandler is heard to say:

"If I go through with this, I win big-time. There's no way I lose. I will get everything I want and they will be destroyed forever ... Michael's career will be over".

During the conversation Evan is asked what effect he thought all this would have on his son Jordan, he replied. *"That's irrelevant to me... It will be a massacre if I don't get what I want. It's going to be bigger than all us put together... This man [Jackson] is going to be humiliated beyond belief... He will not sell one more record"*

Michael's dreams were under threat, the most vicious allegations were being made against him, he felt betrayed and disillusioned that the dreams he had had of ensuring that deprived or sick children had the chance to enjoy some of the magic of Neverland was crumbling. The police searched Neverland and even spent 25 minutes searching Michael himself, trying to match the descriptions of the singer's private parts to those given by Jordan Chandler. They concluded that the description could not conclusively be confirmed. Michael, it is reported, never recovered from the humiliation of that examination.

The tabloid newspapers were having a field day. They painted Michael in a very negative light and there were many complaints that they were displaying blatant bias against Michael Joseph Jackson. Michael was bruised and battered from the mauling he had received at the hands of the press and those who had tried and found him guilty without bothering with any of the evidence. His health was suffering and he finally settled with Jordan Chandler's family for 22 million dollars. The case was dropped due to lack of evidence. Most men would now just fade into the background, give up their dreams and hopes for the future, grateful just to live an anonymous life, but not Michael Joseph Jackson. In 1994, he married the daughter of another American icon, Lisa Presley, the daughter of the legendary Elvis Presley.

Lisa Presley had been by his side throughout all his tribulations, never doubting his innocence. She had been a tower of strength and her belief in him had never wavered. The couple married in secret in the Dominican Republic and, despite rumours that they had tied the knot, continued to deny it for the following two months. The media, however, were not about to let Jackson off the hook and accused them of marrying just to prop up Michael's public image. Although the marriage did not last, ending in divorce two years later the couple were still friendly.

Holding onto his dream, Michael buried himself in his music again, and released a double album *History: Past, Present and Future* became the best selling multiple disc of all time with 40 million units sold worldwide and a Grammy nomination for best album.

In 1996 Michael married dermatology nurse Deborah Rowe and together the couple had two children, Michael Joseph Junior who is more commonly known as Prince, and then Paris Michael Katherine. The couple had built up a strong bond over the years as Deborah had helped Michael deal with his vitiligo and had also become a close personal friend and support. The marriage, however, did not last, but when they divorced three years later, Deborah gave the custody of the children to Michael. She knew how much it meant to her husband to be a father, indeed it was a dream that Michael had cherished for a long time. Now with his son and daughter another of his dreams had been realised.

His musical career continued to inspire the world. It is remarkable that the stormy life of this man never once managed to tear him away from his dream, he held fast to it throughout all the traumas he had, and even when he would happily have spent every waking moment with his children, he still found the discipline to keep his music coming. Through disputes with record labels, the press waiting to pounce on anything they could to discredit him, through accusation about his marriages and even the parentage of his children, Michael held on to his dreams.

In 2002, Michael's second son, Prince Michael Jackson II who was nicknamed Blanket, was born. The identity of the child's mother was not known but Michael said that the child was the result of artificial insemination of a surrogate mother with the singer's own sperm cells. The press had their chance to pounce again in November of that year when Michael, eager to show off his newborn son to his fans, dangled the infant off a fourth-storey balcony, to the horror of the crowd below. Michael later apologised for the incident calling it 'a terrible mistake'.

But life had not finished with the signer yet and in 2003 more child sex abuse charges were laid at his door. In an interview on British TV with journalist Martin Bashir, viewers were astonished to see Michael holding hands with a young boy, Gavin Arvizo, who was 13 at the time, while the pair discussed sleeping arrangements. Seven counts of child molestation and of administering intoxicating substances were brought but Jackson insisted that the sleepovers had never been sexual in nature.

In the torturous two years between the charges and the trial Jackson became depressed and dependent on the drug Pethidine and also lost a lot of weight. The trial started in January 2005 and went on for five months. At the end of it Michael had been acquitted on all charges.

We can only guess at the pain that Michael felt, being wrongly accused of these awful crimes. He had opened his home and his heart to children, hoping to give them a little magic in their lives. In so doing he had left himself open to these accusations, but this was a man who would not so easily turn his back on his dreams. After the court case with Jordan Chandler you might imagine that the singer would never let himself be that vulnerable to criticism again, would never invite children to his home, but he did and Gavin Arviso's case was the result. After the trial Michael left the USA to settle in Bahrain. By now he had financial problems; the cost of defending himself had not been cheap.

Despite this, in March 2009 Michael announced a tour in the UK for later that year. Tickets sold out in minutes, the old magic was still there.

Sadly, Michael never made it to the UK for those concerts. On the June 25, 2009 he collapsed and died. Controversy plagued the singer in death as it had in life, but there was no doubting the grief felt by his fans all over the world.

This was a man who had many dreams and who seemed to be a victim of the very worst of press attention. But no matter how many times they knocked him down, he got up again and held on fast to the dreams and the beliefs he had.

You might think that your dreams are a lot less grand or complicated than someone like Michael Joseph Jackson. Likewise, that may well be true, but like Jackson, you have to hold on, no matter how many times you get knocked back, hold on no matter how many people want to derail your efforts, hold on and believe in yourself when everything looks bleak and even your friends doubt you. Keep your head clear and your heart clean and your eyes firmly fixed on your ultimate goals. Your dream will easily slip from your grasp if you are not careful, so nurture it, tend it, treat it lovingly and hold onto it as though your life depended on it. You need to become part of your dream and it needs to be a part of you.

As we have said before, the dream that you have, the goal or the aim needs to be something that you can actually see. Draw a picture of what your success will look like, what you will look like, what your life will be, where you will be and with whom. Have the details as clear in your mind as your favourite movie. Be able to picture every scene, every person in that scenario, make it your own movie; know everything about it, the colours, the sights, the smells.

Remember every detail, even the smallest detail, anything to bring that dream to life, make it a living part of your everyday life. Something that you can refer to as easily as you could look up a reference in a book.

That dream and those details are what will keep you going when all seems lost, when everybody seems to be against you, when it looks like all your hard work and effort is coming to nothing. That dream that you keep with you all the time, holding on to it and all it means to you, is what will get you through.

Your dream and your ability to stick to it, to treat it like your arm or leg will see you from beginning to end. No one had a tougher time than Michael Joseph Jackson did in holding on to the dreams he had. No one would have been surprised if he disappeared somewhere quietly so that he could live a private life away from the glare of publicity.

Despite the most horrible accusations that were made against him he still came back fighting, the dream he had was too strong to let go.

Your dream needs to be that strong too. If it is and you can hold on to it and live it, you will make it and you will wake up one day and find that everything that you dreamed of is in your hands.

Chapter 5

Swimming Against All Odds

We have talked already about holding onto your dream and having the vision to stay focused when everything and everyone around you seems to be conspiring against you reaching your goal. Even if your journey to success starts well and all your planning and dedication is paying off, a derailment can sneak up on you at any time. This is the time that you will be tested to the utmost, tempted to doubt your own judgement and even your initial dream, forced to confront the weakness in your plan and in yourself. It is a time when sleepless nights and friendless days would make it easier to give up than to go on, when it takes every ounce of your strength of character and belief in yourself to keep going.

What do you do when everything looks hopeless? Whom do you talk to when there is no one who wants to talk to you? Who do you find to believe in you when you have almost lost belief in yourself? The phrase 'swimming against the odds' makes us picture someone swimming against an overwhelming current so that it takes all their strength to keep from being swept away, let alone make any progress. But this is exactly what you will have to do, find the strength to swim against the most overwhelming difficulties and not only to hold your own but to force your way through. If you can do this — and you can — you will SUCCEED!

Apartheid: Nelson Rolihlahla Mandela's Story

There can be few more important and impressive examples of 'winning against the odds' than Nelson Rolihlahla Mandela. A man who is known all over the world and has been an inspiration to so many. A man whose story is so incredible, that you could be forgiven for thinking it was a work of fiction. A man who went from being a prisoner, the lowest of the low, locked away from society for 27 years, to the first black man to lead his country. His given name at birth was Rolihlahla, which means 'troublemaker'. It was his teacher who gave him the name we all know him by today, Nelson.

Nelson Rolihlahla Mandela was born on July 18, 1918. His father had four wives and Nelson was one of 13 children, a child of the third wife. When Mandela was nine his father died of tuberculosis and he became the ward of the Thembu Regent, Jongintaba. The boy was sent to the Mission school next to the palace of the regent. He went on the Clarkebury Boarding School where he completed his Junior Certificate in two rather than three years. Mandela's father had been a privy councillor before he died and young Nelson was primed to take over that role.

In 1937, Nelson moved to Heald town and to the Wesleyan College in Fort Beaufort, which most Thembu royalty attended. He was an active student and enjoyed boxing and running.

Mandela studied for a BA and it was there that he met Oliver Tambo. The two men became life-long friends and colleagues, but at the end of Nelson's first year he became involved with the Students' Representative Council boycott of the university's policies. He was dismissed from Fort Hare and told never to come back unless he changed his views. But worse was to come, as now it was announced that he would have an arranged marriage. Nelson ran away to Johannesburg. The first job that Nelson found was a security guard at a mine, but once his employers found out that he was the runaway ward of the Regent, he was quickly dismissed. He completed his BA at the University of South Africa. He then went on to the University of Witwatersrand and it was here that he met and befriended fellow students who would, like Nelson, go on to be anti-apartheid activists.

Nevertheless, it was after the 1948 election of the Afrikaner dominated National Party that supported the policy of apartheid and of racial segregation, that Nelson began to participate more actively in politics. He was a prominent leader of the Defiance Campaign led by the ANC in 1952 and again in 1955, the Congress of the People whose adoption of the Freedom Charter became the basis of the anti-apartheid cause. During this time, Nelson and his friend Oliver Tambo ran a law firm that provided low-cost or even free counsel to the many blacks who could not afford attorney representation. Life for Nelson was difficult as he himself tried to survive while working for free for others, but he was to become very used to swimming against a tide of suffering for his beliefs.

Mahatma Gandhi and his philosophy on life and fairness influenced Nelson in his thinking and his approach to life. This thinking was to influence succeeding generation of South African anti-apartheid activists.

Although Nelson was initially committed to resistance by non-violent means, he and 150 other activists were arrested in December 1956 and charged with treason. The lengthy trial took place over five years and eventually all those accused were acquitted. But this incident gave rise to those who had a less peaceful approach to protest and a new class of black activists known as the Africanists began to take more drastic steps in their resistance to the National Party, disrupting the work of the ANC in the townships.

In 1961 Nelson became the leader of the ANC's armed wing and became involved in sabotage campaigns against government and military targets, even going so far as to plan a guerrilla war if other action failed to put an end to apartheid. Under Nelson's leadership the sabotage campaign hit at the targets that were seen as the backbone of apartheid such as magistrate's courts but were conducted in a way that no-one was killed or even hurt. Such was his conviction, his belief in himself and his cause that Nelson orchestrated this armed campaign although he must have known what the consequences for him would be and that it was, in all likelihood, a case of 'when' he was caught rather than 'if' he was caught. And on August 5, 1962 Nelson was arrested after being on the run from the authorities for nearly a year and a half. Nelson was sent to prison for five years. Now his swim against overwhelming odds had begun. He was quoted as saying:

"During my lifetime I have dedicated myself to the struggle of the African people. I have fought against white domination, and I have fought against black domination. I have cherished the ideal of a democratic and free society in which all persons live together in harmony and with equal opportunities. It is an ideal, which I hope to live for and to achieve. But if needs be, it is an ideal for which I am prepared to die."

Stuck in prison there was nothing he could do to advance the cause that he felt so strongly about and for which he was willing to give up his personal freedom. But Nelson was not forgotten in his struggle and despite spending 27 years in prison for his convictions throughout all those long wasted years he was revered. He endured the most basic of conditions, performing hard labour in lime quarries and being allowed, as a category D prisoner, only one letter or visit every six months for his anti-apartheid ideals. When he was finally released from prison in February 1990 he became the catalyst who led the way towards a multi-racial South Africa.

Chapter 5

There was still a long and hard swim against the odds to overcome the resistance and violence towards the newly integrated South Africa but in April 1984 the ANC won the first multi-racial election and Nelson became South Africa's first black president. During the relatively short time that this remarkable man was free in society he won more than 250 awards including the Nobel Peace Prize in 1993. This is a man who had a truly remarkable life. His dreams were a long time coming to fruition, 27 long years in prison when Nelson must have had moments when he doubted himself, but he did not give up and even when he was classified not only as a prisoner but as the lowest category of prisoner in the toughest prison in South Africa, his convictions carried him through and he was ready, when he was released, to see his dream come true.

It is hard to imagine what it would be like to spend 27 years of your life in prison. How would you keep yourself motivated? How would you have the strength left to make such an impact on your country and the lives of millions after all that time shut away from society? Well for you to succeed you need to understand the driving force that kept this remarkable man of our times swimming against all the odds, fighting for what he believed in, making a success of a life that had been spent for the most part in prison. When in prison he might have thought that everyone had forgotten about him, his message, the cause he had given up his freedom for, and in your darkest times, it may seem that way to you too. You might feel that the shining dream that you started with has become tarnished, that no-one is going to be interested or support you, or want to hear what you have to say, or buy what you have to sell. That is the time that you need to keep the example of this courageous and quietly spoken man in mind, a man who sacrificed so much for what he believed in.

In addition, your sacrifice, although maybe not of global significance, will make you stronger and deepen your belief in yourself and your dream. That hard swim against the odds will strengthen your arms for the weight you need to carry. The weight of responsibility for yourself and those who depend on you and the determination that you have to carry to its fruition, your dream deserves all your strength, your effort and your struggle against the odds. You have to believe in yourself before anyone will believe in you, you have to have the utmost faith in your dream if you're to be able to sell it to other people. And on that hard swim against the odds, you have to ignore that inviting cove or floating raft to cling to, and keep going, because if you stop you will be swept backwards. And as that tide sweeps you back, you will be undoing all the gains you have made. As the tide sweeps you back you will be able to wave goodbye to the dreams that are on the river bank, the goals that you have achieved, the people that you have disappointed.

No, there is no option where swimming against the odds and the tide is concerned, you have to keep going, even when all your strength has gone, even when you have weights tied to your ankles, keep going, you do have the strength within you, keep your eyes on your prize and your heart and mind strong and that onslaught of power in your way will part to let you through. Take your mind off your aching limbs, your physical and mental discomfort and raise the bar and your expectations. Keep your dream alive and keep swimming against every tide until you reach the goal that you so richly deserve. It may take longer than you thought, it will undoubtedly be harder than you thought but you know that it is worth waiting for, working for and believing in. You know that every stroke you make swimming against those odds, is a stroke that will make you stronger in the end, able to withstand anything that life has to throw at you and make your ACCOMPLISHMENT come to reality.

Gender Discrimination

We have talked a lot about the struggle to succeed and to make our way in the world, assuming that we are on a level playing field. But what if you are a woman trying to make it in a male dominated area or a man trying to make it in a female area of endeavour? One of the last unspoken prejudices is that of gender discrimination, and, by the very nature of the fact that no-one wants to admit that it exists, is one of the hardest hurdles to overcome.

What if the path you want to follow has only been walked by men, and the gates and fences along the way are designed to keep you out and knock you off track? It is a daunting prospect. What if the career and the course you have chosen is predominantly undertaken and dominated by women? What if you not only have to battle against the odds to succeed, but to do it from under the mantle of unspoken gender prejudice? It would be enough, indeed, undoubtedly has been enough, to put many people off, but will you be one of them? Or will you stick to your ideals, hold onto your dreams and keep your eyes on the far horizon of your success?

Legislation exists to prevent gender discrimination but if an employer is set on employing a man, he will do just that, using any number of mitigating reasons for his choice, none of which will be that he did not want to employ a woman!

So do you have to be better than a man or more competent than a woman if you want to break into the preserves of a male or female-dominated world? You bet you do! You have to be the very best you can be, but hold on a minute, don't you have to be that anyway to succeed? Yes you do, so while you are being the best, achieving the most, and overcoming the odds, you might as well take on gender discrimination while you are at it! Don't ever give up just because no-one of your sex has been successful in your chosen career, sweep away any thought of being unsuccessful for any reason, especially your gender, and go for it!

Margaret Hilda Thatcher's Story

There is one lady who springs to mind every time that we think about a woman succeeding in a man's world. That woman is Margaret Hilda Thatcher. A member of parliament in what was in her day, very much an 'old boys' club', how did she become the first and so far only female prime minister of the UK?

Margaret Roberts was born in 1925, the daughter of a shopkeeper from the East Midlands in England where she lived with her father, mother and older sister in a flat above one of the shops that her father owned. Margaret's father, as well as being a lay preacher, was an alderman so Margaret was exposed to politics from an early age as her father, a liberal, ran for local government office as an independent.

Margaret's childhood was unremarkable and although she worked hard at school she was never identified as a brilliant child. She applied for a scholarship to attend Oxford University and was only given it when the original scholarship holder pulled out. At university she studied chemistry and in 1946 she took her first political office as president of the Oxford University Conservative Association.

When Margaret left university and started work she joined her local Conservative party and began her long climb to the top political office of the land. Her chance came in 1949 when a friend told her that the Dartford Conservative Association in Kent were looking for a candidate to put forward as their Member of Parliament. Margaret moved to Dartford, was selected and went on to fight elections in 1950 and 1951 against a 'safe' Labour candidate whom she failed to defeat although she reduced his majority by 6000. Her gender was already becoming an issue as the media took a great interest in her as the youngest ever female Conservative candidate. By this time Margaret had met her husband and Denis Thatcher, a wealthy businessman, funded Margaret's studies for the Bar. Margaret qualified in 1953 and specialised in taxation. Margaret was becoming a busy and influential woman and the same year as her qualification in law she had twins, Carol and Mark. The downside of her success was that her youngsters were often left in the care of nannies. Her daughter Carol recalled:

"My mother was prone to calling me by her secretaries' names and working through each of them until she got to Carol"

Life was getting busier for the fledgling politician and she was finally to enter the House of Commons as the Member for Finchley in the 1959 elections. But Margaret was no 'yes woman'. Despite the constant battle with the 'old boys' club' that she had joined she voted in favour of restoring birching, a stance that was against the official line of her party. Despite this she was promoted to the front bench in 1961 and really began to make her mark. There were undoubtedly men in the party who had a wary eye on Margaret and resented her rise through the ranks but she was a well-bred lady and could fix anyone with a steely look that belied the gentle smile on her face, and make them think twice about crossing her.

Margaret had backed several of her male colleagues to become leader of the Conservative party, but finally in 1975 she put herself forward as a candidate and was elected as the leader of the Conservative party who were not at that time in office. In the 1979 elections she became the first and so far only female Prime Minister of the UK. Cartoon vilifications and unkind nicknames abounded, her speaking voice was ridiculed and every aspect of her appearance from her hairstyle to her shoes was dissected. It is hard to imagine that a man would have come in for the same personal scrutiny. We will never know how this affected Margaret Hilda Thatcher. It is true that politicians have to be, by the very nature of their career choice, thick-skinned, but the press and the impersonators were merciless. Margaret rose above it all, but it must have hurt.

Margaret began to work on her image, most specifically her voice and the way she came across on screen.

"The hang-up has always been the voice" wrote the critic Clive James in *The Observer* newspaper. *"Not the timbre so much as, well, the tone — the condescending explanatory whine which treats the squirming interlocutor as an eight-year-old child with learning deficiencies."*

A clip from May 1973 demonstrating the Thatcher sneer at full pitch was played. She sounded like a *"cat sliding down a blackboard."* James concluded.

She worked to change this image and James eventually acknowledged; *"She's cold, hard, quick and superior, and smart enough to know that those qualities could work for her instead of against."*

Surely, no man in the same high office would have come in for such criticism or would have had to resort to elocution lessons to make themselves more 'user friendly'. The very notion would have been laughable, from Winston Churchill and his mumbling delivery to Harold Wilson and his Northern twang, all had been allowed to speak just the way they wanted to. It was yet another hurdle that Margaret had to jump purely because she was not a man.

Margaret did what she thought was necessary to make

people take her seriously but she had higher goals in mind and set about pushing through her political philosophy and economic policies that emphasised deregulation, in particular with regard to the financial sector, more flexibility in labour markets and the selling off of state-owned companies. But this was a time of inflation and high unemployment figures. It is often said that a war can be the making of a leader, and so the Falklands War proved to be for Margaret Hilda Thatcher. With the country at war on a small group of islands on the other side of the world, support for the Prime Minister grew and her popularity rallied so that in 1983 she was re-elected.

Margaret Hilda Thatcher was well known for her hard stand against the unions, another male-only preserve in the United Kingdom and she refused to give in to them despite strikes that all but paralysed the country. She escaped an assassination attempt when a hotel in Brighton that she and other Conservatives were staying in for their Annual Party Conference was blown up. She took a firm stance with the Soviet Union and earned herself the nickname 'Iron Lady'. Her tenure as Prime Minister of her country was the longest since Lord Liverpool in the early 19th century. She resigned in 1990 and was made a Baroness, entitling her to a seat in the House of Lords. She split the country; there were those who loved her and those who hated her, those who admired her political ideals and those who blamed her for many of the ills of the country for years after her tenure as the country's first female Prime Minister had come to an end. But love her or hate her, no-one can take that title away from her and her strength and self-sacrifice to serve her country could not be denied. Some said that she was tougher, harsher, less compromising than any man in her office would be, well maybe that is true, and maybe it had to be. Whatever view of her was held there was usually a grudging if entirely unspoken respect for the woman who had made it in a man's world and who had achieved more than most men in politics could ever hope to achieve because, not despite, the fact that she was a woman.

In our struggle, we may come across gender discrimination and we may have to take the hits, the insults, the teasing and outright hostility that is borne of ignorance and fear.

However, if our aim is true and our course is straight we will be able to brush these hurts aside and not let them divert us from our course. We must believe in ourselves before others will believe in us and we must never lower ourselves to the name-calling and insults that others may use against us. To maintain dignity and belief in yourself is the strongest weapon that you can have in your arsenal. With the shield of dignity and the armour of self-belief, all those derogatory comments designed to injure you will simply bounce off you, leaving you strong and whole. It is hard to imagine that there are still people who think that women should not follow certain professions or that men are cissies for wanting to do what have been traditionally women's jobs. It is hard to believe but it is true, they exist and are waiting to knock you off course with their hurtful comments and dire proclamations of what happens to women in 'men's' jobs and vice versa. Listen to them politely and thank them for their concern, their interest in you, and then strengthen your resolve to make your way to your goal in the only way that you know, wholeheartedly, with confidence, dedication and determination.

As you progress step by step towards the goal you have set for yourself, they will fall away, the doubters and detractors, silenced by your success and you will be gracious, never say 'I told you so', always be polite and show gratitude for the most grudging of praise. Remember that underneath your calm and serene exterior you have the inner strength to show the world how successful you can be, how high the mountains you can climb, how strong the current you can swim against. The only thing that stands between you and your success is YOU!

Poverty

So you have your dream, you know exactly where you want to go and what you will do when you get there; only one problem, the rent is overdue, the credit card bills are piling up and you are reduced to eating beans on toast. Is your dream going to remain just that? All your good intentions, brilliant ideas and carefully worked out strategies useless because you cannot get off the starting block, you do not even have enough money to buy a stamp to write and ask for some from your favourite aunt!

Your best plans to make yourself a success and a wealthy success story are stunted for lack of cash, surely this is a hopeless situation, we all know that money talks and without it we are nothing, we fall below the sight line of our fellow man, we are in effect, invisible.

There are not many people who have the strength to pull themselves out of poverty, to overcome a disadvantaged start in life but we have met some in this book, Oprah Winfrey, for instance. Here we are going to look at the remarkable achievement of a man who dared to believe that he could overcome his humble beginnings and make an impact on the world. That man was James Eugene Carrey (Jim Carrey). This funny man had a far from amusing start in life, but he made it, and you can too! No matter what your circumstances, you can motivate yourself to be the winner you deserve to be.

James Eugene Carrey's Story

James Eugene Carrey, one of Hollywood's top-paid funny men, did not have much to laugh about growing up. When young Jim was in high school in Canada, he lived in a camper van with his family.

Things had not started badly for James Eugene Carrey. His father was an accountant but things took a turn for the worse when his father was laid off from work which was when the family had to move into a camper van. Jim had been quite a promising student at school but as the family finances declined, so did his grades, and he worked eight-hour shifts at a tyre factory to help make ends meet. At 16, he gave up his education and dropped out of high school to pursue his passion: comedy.

The life of this young man had all the hallmarks of a wasted life. The fact that the family had been comfortable at one time and, until the age of 14, Jim had lived in relative prosperity must have made it all the harder when his father lost his job and the family fell on hard times. Going out to work in a tyre factory, Jim could have been forgiven for throwing the towel in early and losing any motivation he might have had.

But this young man had his eyes on the prize and his sights firmly fixed on Hollywood. So he took a big risk and moved to Los Angeles where he caught the eye of Rodney Dangerfield, a Hollywood legend. Jim started to make regular appearances at the Comedy Store in the early 1980s and eventually became the opening act for Dangerfield. His career path was set, his luck was in, and the rest they say is history!

So how much does luck play a part in what happens in our lives? Yes it is true that James Eugene Carrey had lucky breaks when he got to Los Angeles, a city that is well known for breaking hearts and destroying dreams. What made this young man from Canada think that he could make it where so many others had failed? How did he find the confidence in himself to make the trip and throw himself on the mercy of such an unforgiving town? After the early knocks he had suffered in his young life and the hard times that he had suffered working in the tyre factory, what gave him the strength to break out of what was the life that he seemed to be destined for? And for what so many would have considered a pipe dream? Comedy is well known to be a difficult area to succeed in. We can only imagine the conversations that went on in the family's camper van as Jim announced his intention to strike out for the bright lights of Hollywood.

Therefore, even if at the moment things are looking bleak for you and you cannot see a way forward, take your strength from reading about Jim. If you believe in yourself enough and if you stay true to your dreams, you will find a way. Open your mind to all possibilities and open your heart to the inspiration and the strength that you need. Read and get more knowledge and information on your dreams and follow those who had made it in that area. As you are persistent, you will find that little glimmer of light, that tiny foothold that will help you on the first step to your success. First you have to believe you can do it and then you have to find a way to get started and then to keep going. A tall order? It may look that way from under that pile of bills that need paying but as long as you don't allow your spirit to be crushed, as long as you keep your head up and your mind focused you will find a way, work out a path, beg or borrow the money you need in the sure knowledge that you will be able to repay tenfold when you finally realise your dreams and goals.

The only limiting factor to your success is you. This book is full of inspirational stories of people triumphing over prejudice, discrimination, poverty, almost any handicap that you can imagine. To those people failure was not an option and whatever they had to overcome, they overcame, however high the mountain they climbed it and however wide the sea, they swam it. They did not sit at home feeling sorry and expecting a pity party for themselves, and saying that it was all a hopeless pipe dream. They refused to be held back by mere money or any other limiting factor, and if you want to be a success, you will have to have the same can-do attitude, the same refusal to admit defeat, see failure and setback as stepping stones and the same determination to flourish.

Health Challenges

There are times in this life when you see someone who has made it despite overwhelming odds and you think to yourself, how did they do that? Having no money or a lack of motivation can be overcome. Even prejudice can be overcome, but a permanent disability is another thing. In a society that values beauty and physical perfection seemingly above all else, how can we make our mark against the odds. Newspapers and magazines are full of photographs of apparently flawless celebrities baring their immaculate flesh for us all to see and aspire to. In the entertainment industry this is especially true and Los Angeles is a prime example of a culture that worships perfection. Everyone there is slim to the point of anorexia, surgically enhanced and kitted out in clothing a single piece of which would cost most people a month's salary. Anyone in the celebrity world who gains a few pounds can expect hoards of drooling paparazzi to be staking out their next beach holiday; eager to snap a less-than-flattering shot of them bulging in a bikini to display in print with shock headlines that would make you think they had grown another head rather than gained a few pounds. Even the most magnificent tribute to those who have triumphed over adversity, the Paralympics attracts many less followers than the Olympics contested by able-bodied athletes.

So does that mean that if we are less than perfect we should not aspire to greatness? No, it does not! In this chapter, I would like you to look at someone who made it in spite of setbacks and disabilities that would have made many people give up before they even started.

Stevie Wonder's Story

The name Stevie Wonder must be one of the best known in the world. His music has been an inspiration to many musicians and his songs are loved by millions. Stevie Wonder was born in 1950 six weeks prematurely at a time that there were not the resources available for premature babies that there are today. In fact, it is a miracle that he even survived. One of the recognised complications of premature birth is that the eyes have not finished developing. This was the case for Stevie and although he has reported that he thinks he can vaguely remembers light and what his mother looked like even that he says might have been the product of a dream.

Stevie was one of five children brought up single-handedly by his mother in inner city Detroit. There is no doubt that his early life was hard and money was very tight. There was little in his early days to inspire or encourage the young blind Stevie but he has said that as a child he soothed his mother's tears by telling her that he "wasn't sad." He recalled, "I believed God had something for me to do."

He and his brothers and sister joined the local Baptist choir and despite his blindness, by the age of 11 Stevie had shown a talent for playing piano, the harmonica and the drums. The hand of God, through a friend of Stevie's, delivered Wonder's fate into the hands of Berry Gordy who was the president of Motown Records. Gordy placed the exceptional young man's career in the hands of his associate Clarence Paul, whom he designated as Wonder's mentor. Gordy told Paul that his job was to "bring out his genius. This boy can give us hits." Stevie was handed the showbusiness name 'Little Stevie Wonder,' and the legend was born.

Because he was unable to attend a regular school because of his music schedule, in another miraculous leg up for the young blind boy, Stevie was sent to the Michigan School for the Blind at Motown's expense.

"Motown meant discipline to me" he has been reported as saying. *"The attitude was 'Do it over. Do it differently. Do it until it can't be done any better."* Under such a demanding schedule the young performer grew up fast and he finally put aside the 'little' label in 1964.

However, Stevie Wonder's struggles were not over. When he turned 21, he was due to receive the money he had earned as a minor through an arrangement that had been set out in a previous agreement. Nevertheless, of the $30 million dollars he had made, Motown get for himself a unique degree of artistic and financial autonomy.

"At 21, Stevie was interested in being treated well and in controlling his life and in presenting his music, and all those things were extraordinary things for a young man to ask at that point," explained Stevie's long-time attorney, writing in the *New Yorker "It wasn't the freedom to be dissolute or uncontrolled. He wanted to be free so that he could bring the best of himself to the table."*

It must have felt to Stevie at times that he was very vulnerable, being misused. It must have been a very depressing time, thinking that despite or maybe because of his disability, he had been misled and almost cheated out of what he had earned.

And still life had yet more tests for Stevie Wonder. Stevie's career was almost stopped for good by a car accident in 1973 that nearly killed him and left him with deep facial scars. If anything, however, being the strong character that he was, this event, far from making him give up, gave him even greater focus. Almost all of Stevie's work during the early to mid-1970s was pop, most notably his albums *Talking Book, Inner visions, Fulfillingness' First Finale* and the epic *Songs in the Key of Life.* Some of his most memorable songs from that period, including *Superstition* and *Higher Ground, Boogie on Reggae Woman,* and *You Are the Sunshine of My Life,* These songs were and remain unrivalled both artistically and commercially.

"What artist in his right mind," reflected singer-songwriter and soul icon of the time Marvin Gaye to *Rolling Stone's* Ritz, *"wouldn't be intimidated by Stevie Wonder??"*

In addition, which of us reading his story could fail to be awed by his eternal optimism and determination that kept him going through so many problems in life? To be born with little sight and then to lose all sight would be enough to stop most people in their tracks, but not Stevie Wonder. He knew that God had a mission for him and he kept faithful to that. Then despite the fact that no doubt his record label, Motown Records had done very well out of the young star, he had to fight tooth and nail to get what was rightly his. It is hard to imagine how hurt he must have felt, how betrayed and how sad to have to resort to get what was owing to him by legal action. I am sure that all the time he was working with Motown Records he was treated very well, and spoken to in encouraging and supportive tones. Take a minute with me to look behind the headlines and imagine the shock and feeling of betrayal the young blind boy felt when he realised he was going to have to have a legal battle with the very people he trusted. It takes real strength to fight these fights especially against people you trust but it is a strength that you will have to find and keep if you are going to succeed. You will learn, if you have not already, that people that you trust can surprise you and unfortunately, especially in this day and age, you have always to be prepared for that. At the same time if you make sure that your words and actions are above reproach you will never have to defend yourself to others. To expect fairness one must always be fair, to expect trust one must be trustworthy and to keep from being cheated, one must always be wary.

As Stevie Wonder lay in his hospital bed fighting for his life following his car accident, he would have been forgiven for thinking that he could not take any more. But not this man, in fact he emerged stronger and more determined from the experience. That is what we will all have to do if we are going to succeed. In addition, to reach your goals, you have to keep the faith, fighting and ready for new challenges every time we get knocked down. Keep your focus and your passion strong all the time that other people and events try to throw you off track, keep your ideals and your vision of your success bright and alive in your mind. The disabilities that we have may be or may not be as visible to others but they can be just as difficult to overcome, such as nervousness, doubt, shyness, despair, anxiety and fear. Recognise the things in yourself that might hold you back or make a difference to the way you progress and work on them. Do not give in to weakness or obstacles, just keep your focus on your goal and you will be SUCCESSFUL!

Michael McGrath's Story

If you need some motivation and to be inspired by someone who triumphed over the odds, you need look no further than Michael McGrath. Overcoming odds is, we know, going to be part and parcel of our struggle to succeed, and finding the strength and the belief in ourselves is going to be essential if we are to get others to believe in us and in our dream. Many of us will have the belief of our families and friends at least to start us off on our dream, if we are lucky a close-knit and supportive safety net for us to fall into when times get tough. But what if you are the odd one out in your family? What if everyone else is academic and you are not? Moreover, what if everything is going really well and suddenly you are hit with a devastating illness that robs you of the very essence of what you thought your future would be? Do you give up? Do you feel sorry for yourself and fade into the background? Or maybe, like Michael McGrath you just find another way to shine, another way to achieve your potential, another way to take life by the scruff of the neck and shake it!

Michael's life story is one of consistently and bravely overcoming incredible odds and never giving up, looking beyond his family and focusing on what he could do best, by developing the great potentials within him. British-born with Irish and Brazilian blood, Michael has described himself as the black sheep in an academic family, a catalyst for change and a champion of difference. Choosing a more physical outlet for his talents, Michael made history by becoming the only disabled person in the world to have reached both the North and South Poles and this, by any standards, represents an extraordinary example of determination, courage and singular achievement.

At the age of 12 years, Michael wanted to be a professional golfer. At 14, he was invited to play at Junior Wimbledon.

At 15, he dreamt of becoming the General Manager of the Savoy Hotel in London. At 16, he was a keen rugby player (a flanker) at Stonyhurst College, an independent Catholic boarding school founded in 1593 (guided by Jesuit principles), whose motto "Quant Je Puis" (As Much As I Can) is central to McGrath's own Reach Beyond ethos.

Then at 18 years of age, he was diagnosed with muscular dystrophy, a muscle-wasting disease that remains the single biggest genetic killer of children in the world. In that devastating moment, Michael's life changed forever. Today, his greatest power is described as 'his emotional force in connecting with people.'

He is in demand as a sought-after inspirational business speaker. This incredible man travels the world, provoking, stimulating and inspiring all he meets whilst championing his 3M formula for success (based around the brain being a muscle, the body's ability to move and the mind needing to be fuelled by motivation.) Those to whom he has given his inspirational message include the great and the good in both politics and commerce, and Sir Richard Branson, Chairman of the Virgin Group, said of him, *"Michael is an inspiration"*.

When not speaking or consulting, he's raising vital funds and awareness to support The Muscular Help Foundation, a UK-registered charity based near London that offers help for children and young people in the UK with muscular dystrophy via its Muscle Dreams programme, to live a dream or fulfil a cherished ambition. He is the CEO and co-founder and no-one is better qualified than him. He is the best one to inspire and to show how even when his life was so cruelly derailed and all his sporting expertise affected, he still managed to make not just a success but a stunning success of his life.

One of the truly great achievements of this remarkable young man was when in 2004 he successfully led a team to the South Pole. In undertaking this feat that has defeated many an able bodied man he made history by becoming the only disabled person in the world to have reached both North and South Poles. He had reached the North Pole in April 2002. So how did he do it? What are the qualities that you need to undertake such an epic journey with the disabilities that Michael had. Well they are: leadership, trust, a strong sense of self-belief, teamwork and absolute confidence. In the words of Alexandra Shackleton, one of his expedition patrons, *"Michael continually demonstrates, like [her grandfather] Sir Ernest Shackleton, the qualities of optimism, courage, imagination and patience – his polar achievements are extraordinary triumphs of physical and mental endurance, and should serve as a reminder to us all that, in Michael's own words, 'our limits are often far beyond where we may assume them to be."*

Michael McGrath is now a motivational speaker and who could fail to be motivated by his story? Many words have been used to describe his strengths, such as leadership, trust, self-belief, teamwork, absolute confidence and mental endurance. And the message for us in his story is simple. The man who once described himself as the black sheep of the family has won a place in so many hearts for his courage. Maybe he would have become a world-class sportsman if illness had not robbed him of his strength and maybe he would have felt that he had excelled in an area of endeavour that, although not followed by his family, could be admired by them.

As it is, his achievements have doubtless left his family proud and humbled by their son's determination and refusal to give in to his disabilities. His message to everyone both able-bodied and disabled, is that if you want to succeed, nothing will stop you. The challenges he has set himself would daunt even the fittest of men, and yet he was not willing to use his disability as an excuse to sit on the sidelines. The fact that this man has shrugged off the limitations that life sought to place on him and pursued his dreams is an example to us all. His family have no doubt had many sleepless nights worrying about their boy from the time of his diagnosis to the present day but their pride in his achievements is no doubt fierce.

To succeed we will have to have these qualities, sometimes more of one or less of another but all will be needed at some time. Leadership and teamwork are interesting ones as they seem to be opposites. But to be a good leader you must be a good team player as well, and as we make our way to our ultimate goal we will need to rely on others, we will be responsible for other's livelihoods, for their hopes and dreams and whatever context that comes in, it is a responsibility that we must take seriously, it is the bedrock that our future success is built on. Many people have made money through exploiting and using others but this is not the road to take, even if it seems easy, you must show true quality of character and belief in yourself and your ideals. If you are to be at peace with yourself, have faith in God, focus and follow those who have made it, you will accomplish your ambitions and achievements.

Physical challenges

Can you imagine how you would make sense of your life
if you were born without any arms and legs? It is hard
to imagine isn't it? You might think, if someone is born
without them they will adjust, knowing nothing else, but
we live in a world in which everything from doors to cars to
clothes are designed for people with four limbs. With such
overwhelming disabilities, it really is difficult to imagine
how someone could make a success of their lives, make
their time on earth count, become independent and even
help others. It makes the problems we have look small
doesn't it? Maybe we are struggling to find our direction in
life, to make a success of our business or personal life, or
maybe just trying to discover our place in the great scheme
of things. Well, perspective is a funny thing, and sometimes
looking at things from someone else's perspective does not
help in our own struggle, we can't relate to their struggles,
as we are so caught up in our own. But try to imagine your
life without limbs, without sight, or without any of the
physical and mental functions that you take for granted.
Would it take up all of your time just to find a way to
function with your disability or can you look beyond that?
Can you imagine your problems in perspective when you
compare them to the sort of disability that places you so
far behind the start line, that the race may be over before
you have even begun? If you can then you are on the way to
keeping your life on track and your challenges in perspective.

Chapter 5

Nick Vujicic's Story

One man who might well have been written off at birth was Nick Vujicic, born with a very rare condition named Tetra-amelia. The baby Nick was born with both arms missing at shoulder level and no legs but with two small feet, one of which had two toes. Born in Australia to a devout Christian Serbian family, the otherwise healthy infant's disability devastated his parents.

As you can imagine, the life of this young lad with no arms or legs was filled with hardship and difficulties. One of the earliest hurdles was his schooling. Under Australian law he was prohibited from attending a mainstream school because of his physical disability despite the fact that mentally he was completely normal. However, he became one of the first disabled children to attend mainstream school when the law was changed. He learned to write using the two toes on his left foot and with the help of a special device slipped over his big toe to help him grip. And that was not the end of his achievements. He learned to use a computer using the heel and toe method that he often demonstrates in his speeches. He can also throw tennis balls, shave and get himself a drink as well as answering the phone.

But not everyone was so impressed with the courageous young man and he was mercilessly bullied at school. At the age of eight he contemplated suicide when his pleas to God to grow him arms and legs failed to produce the limbs that he longed for. But then a realisation slowly dawned on Nick. People were impressed by what he had accomplished despite his disabilities and instead of asking God to grow him limbs, began to thank him for giving him his life. Nick recalls that a turning point in his life came when his mother showed him a newspaper detailing the achievements of a young man with severe disabilities. Suddenly Nick realised that he was not alone in facing obstacles that would seem insurmountable to many. This gave him the confidence and the push that he needed and he began, at the age of 17, to give talks to his prayer group. This led eventually to the formation of his non-profit organisation Life Without Limbs. A college graduate, a double major in Accounting and Financial Planning, at the age of 21 Nick began to travel with his motivational speaking focusing his talks on teenagers and the problems that commonly troubled them. Although Nick's message is a Christian one he also gives talks to corporate groups. So far the number of people that this remarkable man has shared his message with is over 2 million, over four continents and 12 countries of the world.

Nick has proven that you can be richer than your dad if you set your mind on achieving success. His aim is financial independence and he is promoting his inspirational message through the media of television on shows such as *The Oprah Winfrey Show* and also through books that he has written about his inspirational story of courage and achievement. His first book which had an expected publishing date of the end of 2010 is entitled, *No Arms, No Legs, No Worries.*

The early realisation that he had qualities that people admired, and that made him an inspiration to others, set him on the path to success and showed him that he could lead a productive and inspirational life of his own. And indeed he has surpassed the success of his family members, despite the fact that they had no disabilities, Nick has really earned his place in history and the admiration of all who meet him. His family must be in awe of this man who grew up battling the odds both physically and mentally, and the fact that he has achieved so much in a life in which, with his disabilities, it would have been so easy to give up, and to have everyone else do everything for you. Not Nick. His strength of mind and his determination not to be labelled 'helpless' have shown this man to be head and shoulders above so many others who have all their limbs. His good-natured acceptance of the hand that life has dealt him is an inspiration. So the next time that you think that you can't work because you have a cold, think of this young man and his example, and ask yourself how much you want that success.

And perhaps the title of this remarkable man's book says it all, what would be the most severe of all body blows to us is dismissed with that most iconic of Aussie saying, 'No worries!'

And as you make your way towards your ultimate goal and face the setbacks that we all have to overcome, think about this young man, of the hurdles he has jumped without legs, the prejudices he has wrestled without arms and the faith that he has had in himself, his God and his mission in life to help others. Not for him a life hiding away with his disability, he has put himself out there, taken on all that life had to throw at him. If you want to succeed in life, you will have to face your own problems head on, take your courage in both hands and believe in yourself and the path you have chosen to walk. Besides, when things are difficult and you feel like giving up, think about young Nick Vujicic, the boy born with no legs and arms. Think about what he has achieved and think about what you can achieve; he did it, he triumphed over adversity, overcame the most difficult starts in life — and if he can do it so can you!

Chapter 6

Never Give Up in Life

Courage

There are a few iconic businesses that seem to have been in our lives forever. Have you ever wondered how these giants of our everyday life got started? Ever wondered if you could be the next giant of your age, with a product that everyone has heard of? Does that sound impossible? Well it needn't be! Whatever your idea, your way of making your mark on the world, the only limitations that you have are within you. We have seen how people have made a success of lives that seemed blighted from the outset, people without education, without money, even without health and limbs, and have made it in their own way. So what is your way? What will be your mark on the world, the thing that you will always be remembered for? 'You can only be remembered for what you have done; not for what your father did.' The thing is, if you give up before you start, no-one will remember you, and you won't even be remembered for giving up! Your ideas are good, believe in them and set the ball rolling. Your capabilities are there for you to uncover and to develop. So what are you waiting for?

Col. Harland Sanders' Story

One man whose product is a household name and who has made his name and his product as popular as each other is Colonel Harland Sanders of Kentucky Fried Chicken.

Born in Indiana on September 9, 1890, over the course of his lifetime Harland Sanders came to epitomize the true American entrepreneurial spirit. Harland's father died when Harland was only six years old and he had to help his mother care for his younger siblings. These were hard times with no handouts to help families and it must have been a very worrying time for young Harland and his mother. Part of his contribution to the running of the household was cooking for the family. With no safety net for families who fell on hard times, Harland had to go out to work at the age of 10 and for the next 30 years, he held a variety of jobs ranging from streetcar conductor, a fireman on the railroads, an insurance salesman and a service station operator. While he was operating a service station in Corbin, Kentucky in 1930, Harland began serving food to travellers who stopped in at the service station looking for something to eat. There was no restaurant at the filling station so Harland served food on his own dining table in his living space at the service station. Soon people started coming to the service station even when they did not need petrol, just for the food! Harland took the hint and seized the chance to make something of himself and his food, by moving across the street to a motel and restaurant where he would be able to serve more people. Over the next 10 years, he worked on his famous, highly secret, fried chicken recipe. Likewise, that recipe in its exact original form is still inuse today. As the reputation and popularity of his fried chicken grew, Harland's fame began to spread to all corners of the state of Kentucky. Such was the recognition for his talent and entrepreneurial spirit that he was made a Kentucky Colonel by the Kentucky State Governor in 1935.

Job done, you might think, he was obviously destined for success. But even for Harland Sanders things were not straightforward. In the 1950s a new interstate highway was planned that would bypass Corbin and his restaurant. Realising that his business would be doomed, Sanders sold off his restaurant operations. After paying his bills, Harland had to survive on his $105 a month Social Security payment.

However, Harland was not going to be that easy to put down. He was confident in the quality of his fried chicken, and at 62 years old, when many people may have given up, Harland devised a plan to franchise his famous chicken. In an effort that would have exhausted men half his age, Harland drove all over the country, cooking up samples of chicken for restaurant owners and their employees. One of the men Sanders supplied the chicken commended it so much and exclaimed that "this chicken is finger licking good." And this was how he gave the name with great pride. If they liked the chicken, he would shake hands on a deal that gave a payment to him of a nickel for each chicken the restaurant sold.

The rest, as they say, is history. In 1964, Colonel Harland Sanders had more than 600 outlets franchised for the sale of his chicken in the United States and Canada. That same year he sold his interest in the US company for $2 million to a group of investors. However, he has remained a public representative for the company, his face as familiar as his chicken, and he has also travelled all over the world on behalf of the chicken he made famous. By the time that he died at the age of 90, Colonel Harland Sanders had travelled over 250,000 miles promoting the chicken empire he founded.

Harland Sanders' energy might make lesser mortals feel tired just reading about it. But it is this energy and enthusiasm that you will need to make sure that your message reaches the audience you want it to. People are not going to come to you. You have to draw yourself up, put your best smile on your face and your best foot forward and convince people that they need what you have got. Whatever your message don't lose sight of it, and if, like Harland Sanders, your original plan has a highway built through it, think again and come up with another plan. There is always a way to succeed, even if it is not the way you originally thought of. You are the only one who has the passion and the love of what you are doing that will convert others to your way of thinking. So be determined and definite in what you are doing and let your enthusiasm shine out and inspire all those around you. Never be afraid to change course if you need to, or to change your message, but always be afraid of failure. Give it your best effort and you will SUCCEED!

Failure

So you know what you want to do, but you think that
there are many more people out there better qualified to
undertake the job. Time to give up? Never! It is hard to
imagine that an uneducated man could arguably undertake
the most powerful and influential role in the world. Surely
it couldn't be possible. Could it? And yet it was, believe it
or not, Abraham Lincoln, one of the best-known and most
revered presidents in the country's history who had a sum
total of 18 months' schooling!

If you are doubting your abilities, ask why. Question why
you think you are under-qualified. Is it because you don't
understand the area in which you are trying to succeed or is it
just that people in that field 'usually' have more qualifications?
If it is the former then you might be in trouble.

An understanding of what you are doing is essential;
otherwise many pitfalls can derail your efforts to succeed.
Maybe there are others who are better qualified than you,
but you must have an understanding, from whatever angle.
There is no excuse for not knowing, and you will progress
even if it is two steps forward and one step back, if you get
yourself the proper grounding in your area of expertise.
There is no excuse for not knowing everything there is to
know and in this way you will put yourself ahead of the
game. Slowly but surely is better than no progress at all.

Abraham Lincoln's Story

Young Abraham Lincoln was born to a very poor family of subsistence farmers near Kentucky on 12 February 1809. He was one of three children and no stranger to hard work even from an early age. His life was far from easy and he never forgot the floods that came and washed away all the crops that he and his father had sown. In December 1816, faced with a lawsuit over the title to his Kentucky farm, Thomas Lincoln moved his family to Indiana. There, as a squatter on public land, he erected a 'half-faced camp' a crude structure of logs and branches with one side open to the elements, in which the family huddled behind a blazing fire. Soon a permanent cabin was built and later Abraham's father bought the land on which it stood. Abraham helped to clear the fields and to take care of the crops but never liked hunting and fishing. In later years he wrote of 'panther's scream', the bears that 'preyed on the swine', and the poverty of Indiana frontier life, which was 'pretty pinching at times'. At the age of nine he lost his mother and this was a desperately sad time for the young Abraham. But his father married again to a woman who had three children of her own. In time Abraham would come to call her 'his angel mother' and indeed she showed no favouritism to her own children, treating all in the household the same. It was she that first encouraged the young Abraham to read and, despite the fact that he was needed primarily to work on the land, he did manage some schooling, although in all it amounted to about 18 months of learning!

He more or less taught himself to read and people who knew the young boy recalled how he would walk miles just to borrow a book. It is almost certain that the family owned a Bible and that young Abraham read it avidly. According to Abraham, however, his early surroundings provided *"absolutely nothing to excite ambition for education.*

*Of course, when I came of age I did not know much. Still,
somehow, I could read, write, and cipher to the rule of three;
but that was all."* Apparently Abraham did not read a large
number of books but those that he did he knew thoroughly
which included Parson Weems's *Life and Memorable
Actions of George Washington,* Daniel Defoe's *Robinson
Crusoe,* John Bunyan's *Pilgrim's Progress* and *Aesop's Fables.*

His family moved again to Illinois when Abraham was
approaching 21 with Abraham leading the oxen. Abraham
was ready to strike out on his own. To city people he must
have seemed a queer fish, six foot four and physically
powerful he was much admired for his wielding of an axe.

He talked with a backwater twang and walked with a long
striding lope. He declared that he had no interest in farming
and after trying several trades Abraham decided that he
would study and qualify in law. This he did and started
a gruelling time in his life travelling far and wide across
the prairies. By the time he began to make a name for
himself in national politics, about 20 years after launching
his legal career, Abraham had risen to be one of the most
distinguished and successful lawyers in Illinois. He was noted
not only for his shrewdness and practical common sense,
which enabled him always to see to the heart of any legal
case, but also for his invariable fairness and utter honesty.

After a few near misses, Abraham eventually fell for and
married Mary Todd. Her family were well-educated, as she
was herself and there was opposition to the match.

Abraham himself confided that he wondered if he were
good enough for her. But the pair married and had four
sons, although only one survived to adulthood. Abraham's
favourite was little Todd who was born with a hare-lip and
a lisp, and sadly also died before he matured to adulthood
although he did survive his father. The marriage was not
always harmonious with Mary having severe bouts of

headaches and depression and running up embarrassing bills and throwing very unbecoming fits of jealousy. She eventually was committed to an insane asylum after losing her mind when her husband was assassinated in front of her.

The remarkable life of this most illustrious of elder statesmen of the United States is well documented, as was his death at the hands of assassin John Wilkes Booth which put an end to an exceptional life. But the lesson he leaves us with is unrivalled. This is a man who lived a hard life.

His childhood was tainted by tragedy and can we even imagine what it would be like to live in a shelter made of trees and branches, open to the elements and to wildlife, even for one night? This man had it tough. He lost two of his four sons, had to watch his country go through the most unimaginable turmoil, bearing the responsibilities on his shoulders for decisions that would change the course of his great land's history. His compassion for his fellow man led to him being instrumental in abolishing the slave trade, despite very severe opposition.

There are not many men who could boast such a life as Abraham Lincoln and in your work and efforts to succeed it is perhaps doubtful that you will be called upon to make such momentous history-altering decisions. But the decisions you make for yourself and what will help you to succeed are as important to you as Abraham Lincoln's wise guidance was to his countrymen. Your background may not have included living in shelters in the woods or teaching yourself to read and write and to count, but many of the challenges you face will mean that you have to teach yourself the qualities that you need to succeed. You can never give up, if you don't know it, look it up! Give yourself every advantage and every reason to succeed. Do not accept even the thought of failure. Be clear about what you need to do and do it!

Remember the old saying 'Knowledge is Power'? Turns out that it's true! Give yourself the edge and the advantage by knowing everything you need to know inside out. Never be caught out in a grey area, and never give yourself the excuse that it could not have been helped because you didn't know. It is your business to know! You have to keep going even when everything seems overwhelming, keep going when everything seems to be going wrong, and keep going when everyone around you is telling you that you will not make it. If you believe in yourself and you can keep moving forward, you will accomplish something.

No-one could have imagined, even at that early point in history that a man with so little education could become president of the United States of America. No doubt there were those bitterly opposed to his appointment on just those grounds. After all, there were better educated men in politics, many of them. And they did not speak with a backwater twang and walk like a ploughman! So how did he do it? He kept going, he refused to give in to his limitations, but most of all, Abraham Lincoln believed he would succeed. He believed in himself and in his ability to take on the highest office of the land. What is more, you have to do the same. Believe in your ability, trust in your instincts and you will achieve amazing wealth!

Chapter Seven

It is never too late to make it in life

Latent Potential

Sam was a quiet little boy. His eyesight had been bad since his birth and he wore thick glasses that kept falling down his nose. At school, he was the butt of many Mr. Magoo jokes and on one terrible day, a group of boys took his glasses, stamping them into the tarmac of the playground. Without his glasses, Sam could see very little. He ran into a wall and crouched there until the bell went at the end of the day.

Blood from his nose dripped down onto his shirt but he did not move. He could not — he could barely see a foot in front of him without his glasses. His mother and teacher found him, cold and soaking wet from the rain that had fallen heavily that afternoon. Sam said nothing. Eventually his mother got him to speak and said he had lost his glasses. He knew that things would only be worse for him if he told tales on the boys who had attacked him.

That evening, Sam's mother took him to the doctor. As they waited in the surgery, one of the other children was banging loudly on an old piano that was against one of the walls of the waiting room. Sam crossed to the piano and tentatively reached out his hand. He played a few notes with one hand and then sitting down on the stool played more, this time with both hands. The piano was out of tune and the playing was clumsy, but Sam's mother sat open mouthed. You see her son had never seen a piano before, let alone played one. That night she and Sam's father talked long into the night about what had happened.

They were a poor family and could not afford a piano, but all they could do was to keep food on the table for their three children. Sam's gift was soon forgotten in the hurly burly of life, Sam's glasses were replaced and broken another four times before he left school. His eyesight was worse now and the career advisors had no real advice for Sam. The head teacher patted his mother on the arm and said, *"Maybe he will be useful to you at home; he is such an obliging young man."*

Sam had been at home for three months when his mother saw the advertisement in the local paper. *Piano, free to a good home.* She did not hesitate. Her heart was breaking for her son, and here was the answer. She remembered that long-forgotten day when he had played the piano in the doctor's surgery. All he did these days was to sit staring out of the front room window where occasionally other young people would come to taunt him.

She ran around to the address that was advertising the piano and within days it was delivered to her. Nevertheless, Sam would not play. Such was the misery and despondency of the young man that he had lost interest in everything. For weeks, the piano stood untouched in the parlour. Then one day, on the radio the beautiful strains of Beethoven's *Moonlight Sonata* filled the air. Sam put his head on one side, he seemed to be listening. Then when the last chord had faded, he got up from his seat, went to the piano sat down and played the sonata, perfect to the last note. His mother felt the tears running down her face as she hugged her son.

From then on Sam was rarely away from the piano, his skill increasing every day. The music that he played spilled out of the window of the house to the summer streets outside.

People began to gather at the garden gate watching the young man inside the window with awe. Word spread and Sam received a visit from a professional piano player, who had heard of his talent, but doubted that he could be that good; to play the piano as well as Sam was reported to be playing a child needed to have learned to play as soon as it could walk. Certainly a child with no formal teaching and such recent experience could not be that good. But he was wrong.

Sam was a genius. At first Sam was reluctant to take up the challenge of playing in public, the taunts and bullying of his childhood were still fresh in his memory. But with gentle persuasion he was coaxed to play at a Christmas concert. More concerts followed and in three years this young man, who had cowered by the school wall to avoid his bullies, grew in strength and confidence. The bullies were now a distant memory, he loved his life and his music and he was afraid of no-one. He was ready to take his place on the world stage, and be the best that he could be.

Susan Boyle's Story

You can imagine the scene; maybe you even saw it yourself? Another hopeful takes their place on the stage to try out for one of the world's biggest talent contests, *Britain's Got Talent*. A plain, middle-aged woman in slightly old-fashioned clothes tells the contest's hard man that she aspires to be like Elaine Page, one of the greats of musical theatre and a prolific recording artist. In his customary manner, Simon Cowell rolls his eyes and the gesture says it all: 'another deluded idiot.' He might as well have spoken the words, his expression was so obviously dismissive. Some four minutes later he and the rest of the auditorium are sitting open-mouthed. From the moment that Susan Boyle opened her mouth to the last dying note of the music, everyone sat enthralled, many moved to tears by the beauty of her voice. Afterwards Susan said in an interview for the *Sunday Times: "I know what they were thinking, but why should it matter as long as I can sing? It's not a beauty contest."*

This is a lesson to us all. On the wrong side of 40, there is just no way that anyone would have given her any chance of being the success that she has been. The music industry is for youngsters, right? It takes years to be noticed, right? Wrong. In four minutes on a stage in a performance watched by millions on television, Susan Boyle changed the course of her life. I am not saying that your dreams and goals could be realised in an instant in this fairytale way, but if your reason for not following your dreams or for giving up on them is your age, you need to think again! Susan Boyle's story is unusual, yes, but it proves that it is never too late to put yourself out there and have a go.

Susan was born in Scotland on 1 April, 1961. Her father, Patrick, was a miner and also sang in the clubs. She was the youngest of 11 children. At the time of her birth Susan had been deprived of oxygen briefly and as a toddler was diagnosed as having resultant learning difficulties.

At school Susan was tormented and called 'Simple Susan' by the other children. Despite all this Susan knew that she had a talent, knew that she had been born to sing. As she entered competitions for her singing she must have endured horrible nerves and with her low self confidence, brought about by many years of bullying, how tough it must have been to stand up in front of a room full of people even with her beautiful voice. The preparation and the effort that she put into her singing and in preparing for competitions were completely focused. This was something that Susan knew she could do well, and she was going to do the very best she could. As she left her childhood and all its torment behind she left school without many qualifications but did take a job briefly in a college learning to be a cook. Susan had by this time begun to sing in clubs nearby. Her parents, recognising her talent and her determination to use her lovely voice, sent Susan to a singing coach and, conquering her nerves, Susan even went on to attend acting school, but the main outlet for her singing was always her local Catholic church.

It was still hard for this shy young woman to put herself forward and risk the ridicule that she had endured at school. Susan, however, never gave up her dream of being a professional singer and eventually, after her talent won her several singing competitions, her mother persuaded her to enter *Britain's Got Talent*. Susan almost abandoned her plans to enter the competition but in the end, after her mother had died, decided to go ahead as it had been her mother's wish. Her performance on that memorable night was the first time she had sung in public since she lost her mother.

After her mother's death Susan lived in the four-bedroomed house that had been her home all her life. She cared for her mother until her death and lived there with Pebbles, her 10-year-old cat. Within hours of her appearance on *Britain's Got Talent*, her picture and voice were on the internet and there was no going back. The fascination with her voice and her story and her age seemed to touch people of many nations and of all ages. There were detractors as well, those who thought that she had been an opportunist, a 'Johnny come lately' to the competition, who resented her success. But these people had not bothered to look into the history of this remarkable woman, the pain and the anxiety, the uncertainty, the shyness, the lack of confidence brought about by relentless bullying that she had had to battle with since childhood as she slowly made her way, through her own talent, to the stage of *Britain's Got Talent*.

But Susan was still fragile, that frightened little bullied girl came to the surface again as her popularity grew. At times it seemed that it was all too much for Susan and people began to notice that she would sometimes behave bizarrely. The day after the final of *Britain's Got Talent* in which she had come second, Susan was admitted to The Priory in London. At the time Simon Cowell said *"I didn't pick up on any unduly troubling signs. She was nervous, yes, but no more nervous than Paul Potts had been before his live final two years previously. She understood the significance of the night. Then, during the final show, at the crucial point when the dance group Diversity won, I looked over at her face and thought: 'Christ, she doesn't know how to deal with not winning."* Even the Prime Minister of Britain wished her well and invitations came pouring in for her, one from the White House to attend their Independence Day celebrations. Simon Cowell offered to waive her contractual obligation to go on tour with the BGT show but five days after her admission Susan was discharged and appeared at 20 of the 24 venues of the tour.

Since her initial successful appearance on *Britain's Got Talent*, Susan Boyle has gone from strength to strength, her music is played all over the world and she is a highly prized guest on many a talk show. This shy middle-aged woman has come a long way from her home in Scotland, and her story has only just begun. Early fears that she could not handle the psychological pressure of it all seem to have been unfounded.

The story of Susan Boyle shows us that it is never too late to pursue your dreams and to realise your goals. Whatever your dream, if you believe in yourself and your ability, then others will too. Don't give up and admit defeat before you even start and don't give up because success is a long time coming to you. Do not be afraid to confront and to admit your limitations, and to acknowledge that you are older than others in the field and use it to your advantage. With age comes experience and like Susan you may have a lot of life experience under your belt. Make that work for you, use it to show others that you have lived a life, that you are coming from a position of having experienced life in general and that you can use your age and your life story and most of all your talent to guarantee your VICTORY!

Chapter Eight

Shattered but Not Scattered

Divorce

Marie was a woman who seemed to have it all. She had a great career, looked good for her 44 years and had two children who didn't give her much to worry about. Her work kept her busy and until they left home her children took a lot of her energy and effort. Her husband, Jim, was a kind man, content to be in the background and to lend a strong arm when needed. But his wife was capable, doing well and marvellous with the kids so he was happy to take a back seat. Marie loved her husband whole-heartedly, as far as she was concerned they were working together for the world they had created.

She admired the way he handled himself at work and in social situations, and never had a moment's concern about the strength of their marriage. They still made love regularly and she felt he was the only person in the whole world that she could be completely herself with, off guard and without any pretence. But somewhere in their busy lives, some of the links between them had loosened, and Jim had decided that Marie was no longer enough for him.

Jim started to see other women, prostitutes mainly, and then, as his confidence grew, women that he picked up in bars, colleagues' wives and then, Marie's best friend, Louise. All the while, Marie was busy working for what they were building together, sending her husband loving notes and soppy cards on his birthday, booking romantic little getaways for them and loving him and their life together in equal measure. Her business started to falter and it was Jim that she turned to for help. He did, but not in the openhearted way that she had become used to and Marie began to wonder what was wrong. Before she could speak to Jim, who now seemed distant and distracted, her friend called her in tears and asked to meet her.

Nothing could have prepared Marie for what came next. Louise told her that she had Aids. She had been tested and it was confirmed. Before Marie could comfort her, Louise blurted out the words that would change Marie's life forever.

"I caught it from Jim."

"Jim who?" Marie asked.

"Your Jim."

It may not be possible to describe the sights and sounds of a world falling apart but that was what Marie experienced over the following weeks. She was shattered, horrified, sickened, deeply wounded and almost in denial. This could not be happening to her. But it was. She was tested for Aids. It was positive.

Jim was now far away and Marie could not bear even to think about him. He had taken her world and shattered it, everything she thought she had and everything she had built her life on was a sham. He had taken her trust, her love and her health and ground them into the dust. Her business went under and Marie thought about death almost all the time. Surely anything would be better than the life she had been left with.

But Marie had an inner strength that had lain dormant for this time inside her. Now it pushed her up onto her feet, made her put on her make up and go out and meet people, made her take stock and day by day try to reach a small goal, then a bigger one. Her marriage and business collapse had had a serious effect on her finances and the house was lost. Now in rented accommodation, the old fighter Marie came through.

She had to make a life for herself, start again, and that is what she did. She took her experience and made it work for her. She started a group for women who had been infected with Aids by unfaithful partners. The organization grew, and as its fame spread she was called on to talk all over the country, she was at last at the top of her game again, and the best of it was that she was helping other women get out of the black pit that she herself had been in, to show them that there was a life after such devastating betrayal, that they, like she, could pick themselves up, dust themselves off and start all over again.

We have talked about how the love and support of our family can help us beyond measure as we strive to reach our goals and be the best that we can be. Their affirmation and their belief in us can help us through even the most seemingly hopeless of situations and the most difficult of times. When everyone else has turned their back, the priceless love and support of our spouse is often the only thing left to us.

We have said how important it is to consider our family and our friends in our plans, and to accept that none of us operates in isolation, that what we do and the decisions we take will always affect others. And then perhaps the ideal for some couples would be to work together to build up something created by them both. But what if that goes wrong and as well as losing your marriage or life partner you stand to lose everything that you have built up together? How do you keep on track when your very foundations have been rocked?

Tina Turner's Story

Ike and Tina Turner, for many years were the darlings of the pop world. Their extraordinary talent inspired many and rocketed them to stardom. But behind the scenes things were far from perfect. Ike was a womaniser and a wife beater and eventually Tina left him in 1976. CNN reported: *"In her 1987 autobiography, I, Tina, she narrated a harrowing tale of abuse, including suffering a broken nose. She said that cycle ended after a vicious fight between the pair in the back seat of a car in Las Vegas, where they were scheduled to perform. It was the only time she ever fought back against her husband."*

Tina met Ike Turner by accident. He was already successful in the recording business and she, desperate to sing, hung around the studios hoping for the chance to sing. One day, when the singer Ike had booked to record A Fool in Love was a no-show for the recording session, Ike gave Tina, then called Anna Mae, the chance she had been waiting for to provide the vocal. Ike, however, had every intention of removing the vocal later.

However, he had not bargained for her electrifying performance of the song, and knowing talent when he saw it, he immediately realised AnnaMae's potential. It was Ike who chose the name Tina Turner and when the record she had provided the backing vocals for became a hit, she was given a permanent place in Ike's band as he continued his drive towards international stardom. Eventually they were married in Mexico and Tina's second son, Ike's child, was born soon afterwards. Tina already had one son by a previous relationship.

It was not long before the Ike and Tina Turner Revue was a prized act at R&B venues both large and small all through the early and mid-1960s. In terms of actual hits, there were relatively few, the live stage show generated such energy and excitement that it made their Revue a sought-after booking along with other greats like Ray Charles and James Brown. But the big break came with the release of *River Deep, Mountain High*, which, although it did not make much impact in the USA, was a massive hit in Europe — and the start of Tina's European superstar status. The Revue entered the 1970s as one of the top touring and recording acts, with Tina gaining more and more recognition as the star power behind the group's international success.

Ike, on the other hand, was described as an excellent musician, an extremely shrewd businessman and was credited with being the brains behind the Revue. But he was also described both by Tina and by others who knew him as *a violent, drug-addicted wife-beater who was not above frequently knocking Tina (and other women) around both publicly and privately.* Even although they went on to have hits like *Proud Mary* and the hit that Tina herself wrote, *Nutbush City Limits*, they never really enjoyed any more success as a group and Ike blamed Tina for the fact that his dreams were slipping away from him.

Tina suffered his abuse and violence for years and even attempted suicide before she finally found the courage to end their marriage in July of 1976. In her final desperate escape from Ike, Tina has been famously reported as having only 36 cents and a Mobil gasoline credit card. It is hard to imagine the pain and the humiliation that Tina must have felt in the years of abuse meted out to her by her husband. She must have been bewildered, hurt and so sad that the man she loved treated her so badly. Her confidence in herself as a woman must have been shattered, her ability to trust ground into the dirt. How did she find the strength to go on, to smile and put on a show beside the man who beat and humiliated her? Well for many years she did until she had finally had enough and left him to try and make a future alone, with no money and her happiness and confidence at stake.

But by now Tina was nearly 40 years old. After what she had endured no-one would have blamed her for fading into the background. But Tina was not done yet, not by a long way and by herself she clawed her way back to the top. She could have wrangled for a divorce settlement from Ike but she refused to do that even though she had massive debts to deal with. And then, little by little, eventually Tina managed to overcome the hurt and the betrayal that had been her married life, began to put back the pieces of her life, and open her heart and her mind to her own possibilities. Tina's profile began to rise, and the rest, as they say, is history.

So if the worst happens to us and our foundations are rocked or even disintegrate like Tina's how can we overcome that? We can do it by believing in ourselves, by taking on the half of the dream that belonged to our partner and making it our own, by refusing to be bitter or to blame, as this is merely wasted energy. We can make our way forward following a different path, climbing a different mountain or crossing a different river than the one we thought we would face. We can be sure of ourselves and of our capabilities, show the world that we were good in a team but we are even better on our own, just like Tina did. If we take responsibility for our dreams and ourselves and open our hearts to new possibilities, we will make our way on our own. A little detour here and there is not going to affect the eventual realisation of your dream. Hold tight to that, believe, and understand that however badly others treat you, you still have your pride and you can do it alone.

Life they say is a bed of roses; but for many around the world this is not always the case. Then would you remain, helpless, hopeless, lost in despair and confusion, and fail to take charge of your life because of your surrounding social environment telling you that you are worthless? I encourage you to arise from where you are now and take charge of your life, take a step-up to move forward changing your history for the better. There is a place beyond where you are now where there are great opportunities available for you, which can catapult you beyond your wildest dreams if you can only apply the basic principles of self confidence which will lead you to greatness.

Your life is filled with defining moments, and you must develop a winning attitude to thrive in turning those moments into triumph, which will lead to a fulfilled life. Learn to develop positive thinking, which can create possibilities in daily challenges that you face; develop self-confidence to make decisive decisions, to be scrupulous in planning and to see setbacks as the process to the next level. With adequate preparations, you will make it at any given opportunity.

Bear in mind, you can be remembered only by what you have done, and not what your parents did.

Develop your organisational skills to enable you set measurable and achievable goals and remain focused on your ultimate goal. By developing these winning skills and attitudes, you will achieve success in life.

Great achievers do not inherit greatness, but they develop their:

- Hidden talent

- Mindset

- Focus on possibility thinking instead of the difficulties and problems; see rough roads as instruments to sieve out dirt from life and destiny

- Involvement on strategic time management to achieve desired goals

- Strength diligently, and courageously by working on their weaknesses

- Passion for what they are doing

- Skill by following others who are brighter, more knowledgeable, better connected and more up to date with advanced knowledge through their books, CDs, videos and sayings

- Lives to becoming problem solvers instead of dwelling on what they are going through

- Mind and belief in themselves

- Aspirations to achieve behavioural changes; and make a difference in their lives, and the world around them

- Intelligence and evaluate the level of progress and reinvent themselves.

You are created to accomplish something in life, the realisation of your potential and working in the right steps leads you to discover success.

Success is not accidental, but adequate cultivation of habits, properly worked-out set goals, and diligence adherence to an action plan.

No circumstances should discourage you from achieving your desired objectives. Never give up, keep your head in the air and fight to the end to make a difference in your generation; YOU CAN BE RICHER THAN YOUR PARENTS!!!!!! Be flexible, willing to make changes and alter your course in the face of reality as situations arise either positive or negative.

What really creates the moment others see in the final round in any endeavour are the daily practice, discipline, diligence, consistency and courage to remain persistent. So arise, there is greatness in you, define your life vision and plans to take what you are doing to a new level, for within what you do there is deep scope so follow it through for success is attainable.

"The heights by great men reached and kept were not attained by sudden flight, but they, while their companions slept, were toiling upward in the night."

Henry Wadsworth Longfellow

About the Author

Patricia Orlunwo Ikiriko is a trained counsellor who has worked with different organisations involved in working with young people for over 15 years. She is happily married to Hon. (Evang) Hope Odhuluma Ikiriko and is a mother blessed with two beautiful foster children and their lovely husbands: Naomi Miriam and Peter Izevbizua, and Timiadedike and Piere Sieker, and two biological children: Doxa Chiudushime Ikiriko and Chanan-Christie Mikabuachi Ikiriko.

She holds a graduate Diploma in Psychology, a Masters degree in Education Guidance and Counselling, a Bachelor of Education in Education and Guidance, Counselling and Psychology, and a National Certificate in Education. She is a professional member of the British Psychology Society, the American Counselling Association, and a PhD student in Psychology at the University of Bedfordshire. She is also a mentor at Hertford Youth

Connex and a counsellor in RCCGCOGI, a non-profit
organization in Watford, Hertfordshire.

Patricia Ikiriko has a passion for helping young people
discover their unique and hidden potential to fulfil their
destiny, determine exactly who they are and what they
want, by setting clear, measurable, and achievable goals.
She helps them to create a strategic plan as a signpost to
their destination, and develop confidence in themselves, along
with the qualities of consistence, persistence; and to remain
focussed to accomplish their dream.

Her inspiration for helping in this way was developed as
she watched many young people she had contact with in
her profession go through life with no vision and goals, and
instead get involved with crime.

She vowed to do something to help them take charge of
their lives, and to learn how to develop the right decision
making and goal setting skills, a healthy mindset, to believe
in possibility, and to cultivate adequate habits through
creating an action plan and diligently adhering to these plans
to attain greatness. Moreover, she knows the best medium
for reaching young people and has written this book to
accomplish this goal. She believes this is the means that will
carry these ideas and information to many in this generation.

References

http://www.buzzle.com/article/life-story-and-timeline-of-oprah-winfrey-html

http://en.wikipedia.org/wiki/Cristiano_Ronaldo

Donald (John) Trump forbes.com

http://en.wikipedia.org/wiki/Usain_Bolt

http://allafrica.com/stories/200710260351.html

www.dailymail.co.uk/.../Barack-Obama-The-story-man-holds-nations-destiny-hands.html

http://davidoyedepoministries.org/church-network/accessdate=2010-02-02

http://en.wikipedia.org/wiki/Brian Tracy -

www.motivational-and-famous-quotes.com/brian-tracy-quotes.html Tracy, B. (2009) Flight plan the real secret of success. Berrett-Koehler Publisher Inc.

http://www.enlightenment.org/magazine/j15/robbins

Branson, Richard. Losing My Virginity: *How I've Survived, Had Fun, And Made a Fortune Doing Business My Way*, 1999, Three Rivers Press

http://www.cbsnews.com/stories/2007/10/11/60minutes/main3358652.shtm

home.comcast.net/~motherteresasite/stories.html

www.thehenrynford.org/exhibits/rosaparks/story.

http://en.wikipedia.org/wiki/Goodluck Jonathan

www.dailymail.co.uk/.../Homeless-man-millionaire-writing-hit-symphony--musical-training.html

www.allmichaeljackson.com/biography.html

africanhistory.about.com/od/mandelanelson/.../bio_mandela.htm

www.bbc.co.uk/history/historic.../thatcher_margaret.shtml

www.thebiographychannel.co.uk/biographies/jim-carrey.html

www.poemhunter.com/lyrics/stevie-wonder/biography/

www.nyt.co.uk/michael.mcgrath.htm

www.lifewithoutlimbs.org/

www.ronford.net/ui/kfc3/.../colonel/colhistory1.htm

www.cybernation.com/lincoln/bio.php

en.wikipedia.org/wiki/Susan_Boyle 1

www.imdb.com/name/nm0877913/bio

www.quotationspage.com/quote/1941.html